SUCCESS
secrets to maximize
BUSINESS
in the
UNITED ARAB EMIRATES

Harvey & Margaret Tripp

TIMES BOOKS INTERNATIONAL
Singapore • Kuala Lumpur

National Library Board (Singapore) Cataloguing in Publication Data

Tripp, Harvey.
　　　Success secrets to maximize business in United Arab Emirates /
Harvey & Margaret Tripp. – Singapore : Times Books International, 2001.
　　　p. cm. – (Culture shock!)

　　　Includes index.
　　　　ISBN : 981-232-200-0

1.　Business etiquette – United Arab Emirates.　2. Corporate culture –
United Arab Emirates.　3. Success in business – United Arab Emirates.
I. Tripp, Margaret.　II. Title.　III. Series: Culture shock!

　HF5389
　395.52095357 — dc21　　　　　　　　　SLS2001030104

All photographs by Margaret Tripp
© 2002 Times Media Private Limited
Published by Times Books International
An imprint of Times Media Private Limited
A member of the Times Publishing Group
Times Centre, 1 New Industrial Road, Singapore 536196
Fax: (65)285 4871 Tel: (65)284 8844
e-mail:te@tpl.com.sg

Online Bookstore:
http://www.timesone.com.sg/te

Times Subang
Lot 46, Subang Hi-Tech Industrial Park
Batu Tiga
40000 Shah Alam
Selangor Darul Ehsan
Malaysia
Fax & Tel: (603)5636 3517
e-mail:cchong@tpl.com.my

All rights reserved. No part of this book may be reproduced
or utilized in any form or by any means electronic or
mechanical, including photocopying, recording, or by an
information storage and retrieval system, without permission
from the copyright owner.

Printed in Singapore

ISBN 981 232 200 0

Contents

Acknowledgments 7

Introduction 8

Map of the United Arab Emirates 10

Section 1—Understanding and doing business in the UAE

Chapter 1— From Pirate Coast to the United Arab Emirates 11
Early Settlement 11
European Traders 11
British Protectorate 12
Uniting the Emirates 14
An Oil Driven Society 17

Chapter 2—The Economy of the United Arab Emirates 25
The Dominance of Abu Dhabi and Dubai 25
Exports, Re-exports and Imports 26
A Stable Currency 29
Sophisticated Banking and Finance 30
A Low/No Taxation Regime 32
A Net Creditor Country 33
Disparity of Income 34
An Economy of Foreign Workers 34
UAE Nationals as a Minority in the UAE 38
Increased Competition from Bahrain 42

Chapter 3—The Government 44
    Overview 44
    Lack of a Federal Vision 45
    Supreme Council of Rulers 47
    The Council of Ministers 47
    Federal National Council 48
    The Federal Judiciary 48
    Stable Politics 50
    The Majlis 51
    Emirate of Abu Dhabi 52
    Emirate of Dubai 53
    Emirate of Sharjah 54
    Emirate of Ras al Khaimah 54
    Emirate of Ajman 54
    Emirate of Fujairah 54
    Emirate of Umm al Qaiwain 55
    Emirs and Walis 55
    Business and the Bureaucracy 55
    Government and Business 57
    Chambers of Commerce with Real Clout 58

Chapter 4— Infrastructure 61
    Too Many Modern Ports 61
    Extensive Roads, Highways and Freeways 63
    Airports—Almost One Every Few Kilometres 65
    Getting About 70
    First World Quality Electricity Supply 73
    Sourcing Cost-Effective Water 74
    21st Century Telecommunications 76
    Education 78
    Living in the UAE 82

Section 2 Practical Advice on Doing Business in the UAE

Chapter 5—Evaluating Opportunities 91
   Visiting the Market 91
   Supplying the Globe 93
   Emerging and Developing Industries 94

Chapter 6—Choosing a Business Partner 115
   Overview 115
   Territorial Coverage 116
   The Management Team 117
   Commitment 118
   Business Arrangements 119
   Investors 120
   Branch and Representative Offices 123
   Joint Ventures 123
   Partnerships 125
   Sponsorship and Ownership 125
   Commercial Agency Law No. 18 128

Chapter 7—Business Culture 130
   Overview 130
   Business and Religion 130
   Women in Business 134
   Business Transactions 138

Chapter 8—Strategies for Business Success 156
   Research the Market 156
   The Media 159
   Outdoor Advertising 160
   Trade Fairs and Exhibitions 161
   The UAE's Silicon Valley 161
   Promotions and Marketing 162

The Right Price 162
The Right Product 163
Commercial Laws of the UAE 164
Intellectual Property Rights 167
Business Licence 168
Company Registration 168
Choosing a Business Site 170
Free Trade Zones and Technology Parks 172
Contacts and Networking 177
Corporate Culture 177
Conclusion 179

Appendices
A Basic Facts and Travel Tips 180
B Directory of Important Contacts 184
C Recommended Reading 187

About the Authors 188
Index 189

Acknowledgments

Julie & Roger Bayliss, Chuang KB, Greg Coelho, Tony Collier, Peter Deacon, Kay & Trevor Edwards, Ala Ghanem, Merv Giles, Garry Hall, John Hayes, Tino Karras, Gerald Lawless, Edward Lim, Lynda Mahoney, Jane Monico, Peter North, Lisa Steel, Fay Thompson, Chloe Tripp, Len Tripp, Max & Georgie White.

Introduction

Harvey has had a long association with the United Arab Emirates (UAE) and the immediate region known as *The Gulf*. The Iranians claim it is the *Persian Gulf*, whereas the Arab nations claim it is the *Arabian Gulf*. Before the invention of e-mail, faxes and telexes when a letter was the principal means of written communication, if one were to address a letter to the Emirate of Dubai and include the words "Persian Gulf" on the envelope, there was no guarantee that the letter would be delivered since the Emirate of Dubai believed that the sea surrounding its coastline was the Arabian Gulf and not the Persian Gulf.

In the 1950s, *western expatriate* (a broad definition used in the UAE for expatriates from the US, UK and other First World countries) executives and their families often travelled by sea to take up their contracts in the Gulf. It was as the young son of an expariate executive that Harvey first visited what is today the UAE.

Later, in his corporate life, Harvey made many business trips to the UAE and has seen the emergence of Abu Dhabi and Dubai as major regional centres in the Gulf.

Margaret is no stranger to the region either, having travelled to the Gulf (including the UAE) on a number of occasions. Unusual places that Harvey and Margaret have visited in the Gulf include Masirah, an island off the coast of the Sultanate of Oman, where access can only be gained if one is a member of the Defence Force or part of the signals espionage community, or supplies beer to the island.

Harvey and Margaret's friends and business associates have said, on a number of occasions, that they should write a book about their business experiences in more exotic locations. When they heard that Times was planning to publish a business book on the UAE, they welcomed the opportunity to write it.

There are two sections to this book: the first part deals with the economy, government, and infrastructure and sets the scene; the second section goes into the *nitty gritty* of doing business in the UAE, with tips and practical advice drawn from experience.

The authors have found that transacting business can be frustrating at times but if you get the formula right, the UAE can be a rewarding and enjoyable place in which to do business.

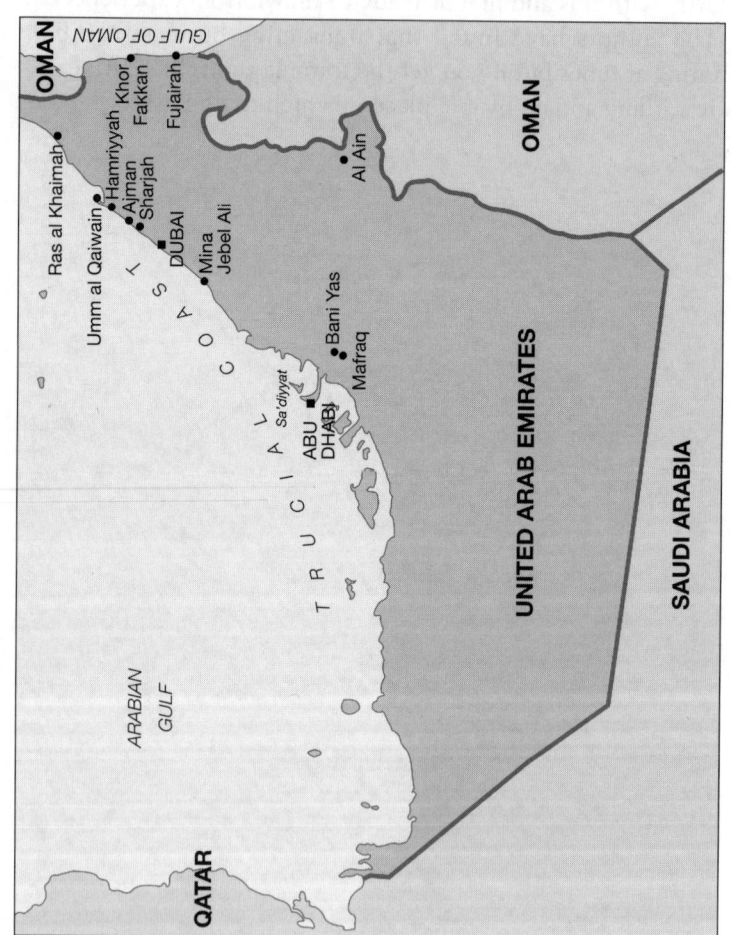

Map of United Arab Emirates

CHAPTER 1

From Pirate Coast to the United Arab Emirates

Early Settlement

Before oil was discovered, there was no United Arab Emirates (UAE): just the *"pirate coast"*. The economy can be traced back to 3,000 B.C. when copper was mined near Al Ain, now the second city in the Emirate of Abu Dhabi, and from the Hajar Mountains. Many crops, including wheat, barley, melon and sorghum, were grown. Historically the Gulf coast, with a number of small fishing villages, was the centre of the spice trade. Overseas trade was mainly with Mesopotania and Baluchistan. Around 2000 B.C. gold and silver were found in what is now the UAE. During this period, principal imports were pottery from India and Mesopotania and glass and coins from the Roman Empire.

Most UAE nationals can trace their ancestry to two tribes who emerged as powers in the 18th century. The Qawasim tribe were land and sea traders who resided in what is now Ras al Khaimah and Sharjah. The other tribe, the Bani Yas, were farmers who lived in what is today Abu Dhabi and Dubai.

Prior to the arrival of the Europeans, what is now the UAE had a significant merchant navy. Dhows, similar to those seen on the Dubai Creek and elsewhere in the UAE today, sailed to faraway destinations that included Kenya, Sri Lanka and China.

European Traders

The Portuguese had a trading presence in the 16th century but were forced to withdraw after they were attacked by a coalition of forces that included the British, Dutch and the Qawasimi. The British East India Company filled the vacuum left by the withdrawal of the Portuguese—but it was not all plain sailing. The ruler of Qawasim had a substantial navy with a fleet of over 60 large war ships and 20,000 sailors at sea, at any one time. The British perceived this naval force to be a threat and set about destroying it. They alleged the Qawasimi were pirates and used this excuse to destroy their navy. As a result, the area became known as the Pirate Coast. In 1853, to guarantee peace at sea, especially during the pearling season, the British made the principal shaikhs along the coast sign a perpetual maritime truce. The shaikhdoms that signed the truce became known as the Trucial States.

British Protectorate

As Britain extended its power over India in the 19th century, it extended its sphere of influence in the Gulf and the Trucial States, making them de facto colonies. Up until 1971, the seven emirates making up the Trucial States—Abu Dhabi, Ajman, Dubai, Fujairah, Ras al Khaimah, Sharjah and Umm al Qaiwain—were British Protectorates, meaning that they were self governing but Britain was responsible for foreign affairs and defence. In each of the emirates, the British Government stationed a Political Agent whose job was to ensure that the policy of the emirate was consistent with British strategy for the region.

The Trucial States were managed from British India and today, the Indian presence in the UAE economy can be seen. An example of this is the number of Indian expatriates working in the UAE.

The economy of the Trucial States was based on trading, fishing and pearling. The commercial capital of the UAE, Dubai, was originally a tiny fishing village. Pearls were exported to India and a market was developing in Europe. At its peak, the pearling industry had a fleet of more than 1,200 boats, each with an 18-man crew. World War I triggered a downturn in pearl exports and this, together with the depression of the 1930s, and the development of the cultured pearl in Japan sounded the death knoll of the industry.

The presence of the British military, with a Royal Airforce station at Sharjah, and the Trucial Scouts (the Trucial States military) provided a stimulus for the economy. At that time, only a primitive airstrip existed. Donkeys carried water and other supplies to the aircraft. The precursor to the UAE government was the Trucial Council, formed in 1952, to harmonise the political and economic policies of the shaikhdoms of the region.

Oil exploration first began in Abu Dhabi in 1939 when the ruler of Abu Dhabi granted a concession to the then British-owned Iraq Petroleum Company. In 1953, a second concession was granted to an Anglo-French consortium for offshore oil exploration. The discovery of oil at Abu Dhabi in 1958 and export of crude oil in 1962 changed everything.

In the lower Gulf, there began a shift of power from Bahrain to the Trucial States and Abu Dhabi and Dubai in particular. Before the discovery of oil in Abu Dhabi, Bahrain was the economic and political hub for the lower Gulf, and also the main transhipment seaport and home base for Gulf Aviation (now Gulf Air)—the regional airline then flying ten-seater de Havilland *Doves* throughout the region, including the Trucial States.

Bahrain was also regional headquarters for the British trading companies such as African and Eastern, and Gray McKenzie. The Senior Naval Officer Persian Gulf had his headquarters in Bahrain because Bahrain had the most advanced port facilities for the lower Gulf. The naval base at Jufair is now headquarters for the US naval forces' Fifth Fleet. Similarly, the Royal Airforce station at Muhuraq was the headquarters for the Senior Air Officer Persian Gulf because Bahrain had the most active civilian airport in the Gulf, and the British Royal Airforce Station was attached to the civilian airport. The British Foreign Office's regional headquarters was also located in Bahrain where the British diplomat, known as the Political Resident, was stationed. There were also Political Agents in most of the emirates. The Political Resident and the Political Agents were, as the names suggest, political advisors to the rulers of the emirates. The Political Residents and Political Agents have long since been replaced with a British Ambassador in Abu Dhabi and a British Consul General in Dubai.

Uniting the Emirates

In 1968, Britain announced its withdrawal from the Gulf and this led to closer cooperation amongst the emirates on the Trucial Coast. In 1970, British military forces withdrew from the lower Gulf, including the Trucial States and Bahrain. British foreign policy was to create a political entity encompassing the Trucial States, Bahrain and Qatar. In 1971, six of the Trucial States confederated to form the United Arab Emirates. The emirates that formed the federation were Abu Dhabi, Ajman, Dubai, Fujairah, Sharjah and Umm al Qaiwain. In 1972, the seventh Trucial State, Ras al Khaimah, joined the confederation.

The old and the new—the Embassy of Kwait and the Department of Commerce and Marketing building are alongside each other.

Country Snapshot

Political Status	Federation
Religion	80% Sunni Muslim
	16% Shiite Muslim
	4% Other Religion
Population Growth	4% per annum
Population Density	29 per sq km (74 per sq mile)
Average Life Expectancy	Men 69 years, Women 75 years
Per Capita Income	US$ 19,270
Oil Reserves	200 billion barrels
Largest Emirate: Abu Dhabi	85% of land mass
Smallest Emirate: Ajman	250 square km, 100 square miles
Political Capital	Abu Dhabi
Commercial Capital	Dubai
Topography	low lying sandy desert with extensive salt flats
Climate	Temperature ranges from 18°C (65°F) in January to 43°C (110°F) in July
Average Rainfall	75mm to 100mm per annum (3 to 4 inches)
Location	Latitude 22°–26.5° N
	Longitude 51°–56.5° E
Borders	To the north by the Arabian Gulf
	To the east by the Gulf of Oman and the Sultanate of Oman
	To the south by the Sultanate of Oman and Saudi Arabia
	To the west by Saudi Arabia and Qatar

Source: *Microsoft, Encarta –1999/UAE Year Book 1999*

Size and Population of Individual Emirates, 1999

Emirate	Area (sq km)	Population
UAE	75,160	2,929,000
Abu Dhabi	64,750	1,127,000
Ajman	260	161,000
Fujairah	1,170	92,000
Dubai	3,900	858,000
Ras al Khaimah	1,700	156,000
Sharjah	2,600	491,000
Umm al Qaiwain	780	44,000

The finding of oil transformed the economies of Abu Dhabi and Dubai and affected that of the other emirates. Propelled by the troubles in Lebanon and the business acumen of the then ruler of Dubai, major corporations that had their Middle Eastern headquarters in Beirut began to relocate to Dubai. Companies which had their lower Gulf headquarters in Bahrain also relocated to Dubai. The 1991 Gulf War prompted more movement as companies relocated further away from Iraq, and from Bahrain which was feared to be a possible military target of Iraq because it was, and still is, home port for the US navy's Fifth Fleet.

In the early days of the federation, there was considerable political rivalry amongst the ruling families of the emirates and, in particular, the rulers of Abu Dhabi and Dubai. Examples of the rivalry can be seen in the duplication of infrastructure. Well after federation, Dubai and Sharjah maintained their own military forces which have now been merged into the UAE defence force. Today, there is a fair degree of economic synergy. The ruling family of Dubai has the business knowhow and the ruling family of Abu Dhabi has the financial clout to make things happen.

An Oil Driven Society

Overview
Oil and gas dominate the economy of the UAE and are likely to continue to do so in the foreseeable future. They accounted for 33% of gross domestic product (GDP), more than 60% of government revenue and 80% of the UAE's income in 1998. The federal and emirate governments have been active in using funds generated from oil revenue to develop other sectors of the economy, for example, infrastructure projects in the 1990s. Other resources include copper in Fujairah and Ras al Khaimah, talc in Fujairah and manganese in the northern emirates. Feasibility studies are being taken to evaluate the commercial viability of extracting and processing these minerals.

Large Oil Reserves
Commercial quantities of oil were first discovered in Abu Dhabi in 1959 (fairly late by Gulf standards) and exports commenced in 1962. The discovery of oil was the catalyst that transformed the UAE from a sleepy Bedouin backwater to the present fast growing economy. Abu Dhabi produces most of the oil, followed by Dubai.

Abu Dhabi In 1971, the Abu Dhabi National Oil Company (ADNOC), with all shares owned by the Abu Dhabi government, was formed. It was given the monopoly to distribute petroleum products and petroleum facilities in the Emirate of Abu Dhabi. ADNOC, in addition to having its own concession and operations, is also an investor and has substantial equity in about fifteen oil related businesses that are structured to form the ADNOC group. ADNOC represents the Abu Dhabi government's oil interests.

Abu Dhabi is one of the few countries in the region that does not have a nationalised petroleum industry. In 1990, the Federal Oil Ministry was downgraded and its powers transferred to the

Supreme Petroleum Council which is responsible for formulating oil and gas strategy for the emirate.

Control of output and production levels for all companies, including the ADNOC group, is set by the Abu Dhabi Supreme Petroleum Council whose chairman is the Crown Prince of Abu Dhabi. The Abu Dhabi Emirate Government has the controlling interest in the oil reserves of Abu Dhabi.

ADNOC has 60% equity in two major operating companies— the Abu Dhabi Company for onshore oil operations (ADCO) and the Abu Dhabi Marine Operating Company (ADMA). Foreign companies have a 40% share in each of these operating corporations. British Petroleum (BP) is the most significant minority shareholder with a 24% stake, Shell has 10% and Mobil Exxon and Partex have smaller shares.

In another venture to operate the reservoirs at the Upper Zakum and Umm al Delkh Field, ADNOC has an 88% equity in the Zakum Development Company. Japan Oil Development Company has the remaining 12%; interestingly, in addition, it also received a share of the oil reserves as well as an offer of the concession in return for a tradeoff where Zakum Development Company would have access to the latest technology.

There are some joint ventures in the smaller oil fields where ADNOC has no direct presence.

In the Emirate of Abu Dhabi, the major offshore oil fields are located at Umm Shaif, Lower Zakum, Upper Zakum, al Bunduq and Abu al Bukhoosh. The main onshore oil fields are Asab, Bab, Bu Hasa, Sahil and Shah. They are all located approximately 250 kilometres west of Abu Dhabi.

It is estimated that the UAE has oil reserves of approximately 98.2 billion barrels that will last until the 21st century, and ranks as the third largest in the world. This translates to 9.5 % of global crude oil reserves. Over 90% of crude oil reserves in the UAE are located in the Emirate of Abu Dhabi which is also the biggest producer, controlling 85% of the UAE crude oil output.

In 1999, 62% of crude oil exports was to Japan, the UAE's largest customer. Other major customers include the US, France and the Netherlands. Germany and the UK are smaller buyers of oil from the UAE.

Oil from the major onshore and offshore fields is pumped to refineries at Ruwais and Umm al Nar.

The marketing of refined products in the Emirate of Abu Dhabi is the responsibility of an ADNOC affiliate, ADNOC Distribution. Most of the offices of the oil companies and related businesses, including the ADNOC group, are in Abu Dhabi.

ADNOC's international arm is the International Petroleum Investment Company which has equity in a number of downstream projects in Europe and Pakistan. Of significance is its 25% equity in Borealis, Europe's largest polyolefins manufacturer.

Other Emirates Dubai is the second largest producer of oil in the UAE, on a much more modest scale than Abu Dhabi. Shipments commenced in 1969 and the financial proceeds were sufficient to transform Dubai from an old trading port to a modern metropolis.

The major oil producer in Dubai is the Dubai Petroleum Company whose activities are focused on offshore production. It operates the oil fields in Dubai in association with strategic allies that include Total, a French company, and RWE-DEA AG, a German company. There are four offshore fields: the Fateh and South West Fateh fields are the largest and the oldest, and the two smaller offshore fields are Falah and Rashid. *Fateh* in Arabic means good fortune. Dubai's major onshore oil field, the Margham field, was discovered in 1982.

The Emirates National Oil Company (ENOC) is responsible for oil and gas manufacturing in the Emirate of Dubai . The actual refining of oil in Dubai is the responsibility of the Emirates Petroleum Products Company, an affiliate of ENOC located in the Jebel Ali Free Zone, which also supplies naptha to the Emirates Gas Company, another ENOC affiliate.

The retailing of refined products in the Emirate of Dubai is the responsibility of the federally owned Emirates General Petroleum Company, formed in 1981 to take over the retail service stations previously operated by BP, Caltex, Shell and the Emirates Petroleum Products Company.

In 1999, Dubai accounted for approximately 30% of all oil produced in the UAE. Oil reserves for the Emirate of Dubai were estimated to be four billion barrels in 1998 and are projected to expire in 2020. Dubai has been preparing for the runout of oil and has diversified the economy to such an extent that, in 2001, oil accounted for only 20% of GDP.

Sharjah also has oil reserves but they are minute when compared with Abu Dhabi and Dubai. Sharjah shares the output from the Mubarak offshore oil field discovered in 1972 with Dubai. Production from the Mubarak field has steadily declined. In 1980, the Amoco Oil Company discovered an onshore oil field close to the city of Sharjah. Oil production in Sharjah represents less than 1% of UAE output. Its 1998 oil reserves were approximately one billion barrels. A refinery in the Hamriyyah Free Zone commenced operation in 1999.

Ras al Khaimah has a small offshore oil field that represents less than 1% of UAE oil output but oil is a major source of income for this emirate.

A small amount of crude oil is refined in the Emirate of Fujairah.

The UAE is a member of the Organisation of Petroleum Exporting Countries (OPEC) and the Organisation of Arab Petroleum Exporting Countries (OAPEC). It is the third largest producer of oil in the Arabian Gulf after Saudi Arabia and Kuwait. In 1999, there were six operational refineries in the UAE. Federal government strategy is to value-add petroleum exports through the movement, away from crude oil exports.

Significant Gas Reserves

Complementing oil in the UAE are significant gas reserves. The UAE is the main producer of liquefied natural gas in the Gulf. In 2001, it had 4% of the world's gas reserves or 205 trillion cubic feet—the fourth largest gas reserves in the world. At the current rate of consumption, this will last well into the next century. Nearly all gas exported from the UAE is to Japan. In fact, the UAE supplies over 10% of Japanese liquified gas requirements. Prior to the 1980s, there was considerable wastage of gas. Visitors taking the night flight to the UAE witnessed the eerie spectacle of flames shooting into the air. Today, the gas has been harnessed.

Abu Dhabi As with oil, nearly all the proven recoverable gas reserves (92%) are in the Emirate of Abu Dhabi. ADNOC represents the government as the owner of natural gas in the Emirate of Abu Dhabi. It formed the Abu Dhabi Gas Industries Limited to manage gas from the onshore fields, and the Abu Dhabi Gas Liquefaction Company to manage the offshore gas fields of the world's largest gas reserves at the Khuff reservoir.

Some of the gas from the Abu Dhabi fields is used to power the Umm al Nar industrial complex and the world's largest desalinisation plant at Taweelah.

Abu Dhabi's main gas plant is on Das Island where propane and butane are produced and exported by the Abu Dhabi Gas Liquefaction Company to Japan. The company has a long term contract to supply gas to the Tokyo Electric Power Company plus other companies in East Asia and Europe.

Other Emirates The Emirate of Dubai had 2% of the UAE gas reserves as at 1999; the principal reserves are from offshore fields. The Atlantic Richfield Company operates the onshore Marghan gas field. In 1999, the Dubai Supply Authority, together with ADNOC and the UAE Offset Group announced a joint venture to develop the Dolphin project. This involved the supply of gas from Qatar to power producers, aluminium smelters, iron and steel plants and petrochemical industries in Oman, Pakistan and the UAE. (The UAE Offset Group is the organisation that manages the UAE government requirement that all overseas companies winning defence contracts invest a portion of profits received in the UAE, in joint venture projects.) ADNOC also has an agreement with the Emirate of Dubai to supply power to the Jebel Ali Industrial Zone. The Dubai Supply Authority is responsible for ensuring that Dubai has sufficient gas for industrial and domestic requirements.

Sharjah, in 1999, had 5% of the UAE gas reserves. All gas produced in Sharjah is consumed in the UAE. Sharjah's main offshore gas deposit is the Mubarak Field and the onshore fields are Sajaa, Mo'Ayyid and Kahaif. The Crescent Petroleum Company manages and operates the offshore Mubarak gas field and has a joint venture with the UK based Atlantas Company to explore for gas reserves in Sharjah's interior desert. BP-Amoco operates the onshore gas fields. The Sharjah Liquified Gas Company distributes natural gas to households and businesses in Sharjah.

The Emirate of Ras al Khaimah has a small offshore gas field called the Saleh field where the product is piped 42 kilometres ashore to provide power to the cement plant at Khor Khuwaii. In 1997, Norway-based Atlantas Technology Services was given a permit by the emirate government to explore the offshore Baih gas field. The Ras al Khaimah Oil and Gas Company has been given the rights by the government to explore hydro carbon opportunities in the emirate.

The oil and gas-rich Emirate of Abu Dhabi has diversified its economy vertically into petrochemicals and other oil and gas related businesses as a defence against unstable oil prices. Its economic strategy is to focus on creating value-added projects in gas and petrochemicals. ADNOC owns a chemical plant, FERTIL, and a petrochemical company. The Abu Dhabi Polymers Company Limited is a joint venture between ADNOC and Borealis. It trades under the name, Borouge. In 2001, it opened a major facility at Ruwais to produce linear low density and high density polyethylene. The plant is one of the biggest producers of polyethylene in the Middle East and will meet the anticipated surge in demand for pipes and films. The opening of the plant created employment opportunities for UAE nationals.

ADNOC also plans to open an ethylene-dichloride complex and an aromatics plant. Products manufactured at the plant will be exported to Asia.

The Middle East is the fastest growing market for plastic raw materials and the UAE is the second largest producer of polyolefins. The growth of plastics in the Middle East is projected at 30% annually for the next five years.

The Abu Dhabi government plans to make a substantial investment in petrochemicals and other downstream oil related products. The objective is to have four petrochemical plants plus the biggest polyethylene plant in the Middle East. The Emirate Investor Company is establishing a plant to produce formaldehyde derivatives such as UFC 85, resins, glues and urea. The project is part of an import replacement programme and the products will also be marketed to the Arab Gulf Co-operation Council (AGCC) countries. The AGCC is a common market formed at a political conference in Abu Dhabi in 1981 by the UAE and other Gulf states which included Bahrain, Kuwait, Qatar, Oman and Saudi Arabia.

The funds generated from oil has enabled the government to raise the living standards of UAE nationals by providing families with free medical service, new homes with modern conveniences and free education. UAE nationals also receive subsidised power and water, financial assistance to start new businesses and free land. Loans often do not have to be repaid.

The status of the economy is very much dependent on the price of oil. As the price goes up, the economy advances. Conversely, as the price goes down, the economy contracts. During much of the 1990s, the economy contracted because of the relatively low price of oil. In 2001, outlook was positive because of high oil prices. In 2000, GDP showed a fantastic growth of 14% when compared to the previous year. The reason—increased oil prices. Crude oil's share of GDP catapulted from 27% in 1999 to 38% in 2000. Although the first few years of the 21st century were good to the UAE because of high oil prices, the government is most anxious to see stable prices to avoid a gyrating economy.

Unlike many of its AGCC neighbours, the economy of the UAE has been cushioned to some extent because of the diversification of the economy away from oil.

CHAPTER 2

The Economy of the United Arab Emirates

The Dominance of Abu Dhabi and Dubai

The economy of the UAE is dominated by the oil produced in the emirates of Abu Dhabi and Dubai. As a result of its oil wealth, the Emirate of Abu Dhabi has all the clout and is by far the largest contributor to the federal UAE budget. The dominance of the Emirate of Abu Dhabi is somewhat resented by the smaller emirates, especially as the ruler of Abu Dhabi is also always the president of the UAE. On the other hand, this is accepted because of Abu Dhabi's financial support to the smaller emirates.

Similarly, because Dubai is the major trading centre and second most important emirate, its ruler is always the vice president of the UAE and almost always the prime minister of the UAE.

The smaller emirates of Ajman, Fujairah, Ras al Khaimah and Umm al Qaiwain receive substantial subsidies from the federal government.

Sector Share of GDP, 2000

Sector	%
Crude oil	39.1
Manufacturing	8.3
Construction	8.8
Trade	10.2
Transport, Storage & Communication	5.5
Finance, Insurance & Real Estate	11.5
Government Services	11.3
Other	5.3
Total	100.0

Exports, Re-exports and Imports

According to the Emirate Industrial Bank (EIB), in 1999, the UAE was the third most important re-export centre after Hong Kong and Singapore. Most re-exporting is done from Dubai. Machinery, textiles and vehicles are re-exported to Iran, and silver and jewellery are re-exported to India. Apart from these two countries, there is a fairly even spread of re-exports to more than 30 countries. Other important re-export markets include the Horn of Africa, Bahrain, Kuwait, Saudi Arabia and the Commonwealth of Independent States (CIS). Approximately 25% of UAE imports are re-exported. There are significant variances in the amount of imports each emirate re-exports. Of all imports into the UAE, approximately two thirds enter through the Emirate of Dubai.

The wide variety of products re-exported includes Indian tea, Japanese video cassette recorders, powdered and evaporated milk from the Netherlands, Chinese wheelbarrows and Korean truck tyres.

Dubai is the supply hub for gold in the Middle East and 90% of all jewellery imported into the UAE is through its port. The main source of gold and jewellery imports is Bahrain, India, Italy, Malaysia, Pakistan, Saudi Arabia, Singapore and Thailand. Gold and jewellery imports are re-exported to other AGCC countries, Iran, Egypt, India and Pakistan.

Over half the value of imported products are consumer goods. Capital goods make up over a third of imports. The UAE government describes the balance as intermediary goods. Categories of goods imported include machinery, transport equipment, manufactured goods, food, live animals, motor vehicles and gold.

Nearly half of all imports are sourced from Asia and slightly more than a third are imported from Europe. The US is the other significant source of imports.

The central business district of Dubai, located in Deira, is the regional headquarters for many multinationals.

Non oil exports have continued to become more important to the economy of the UAE and Dubai in particular. On any one day, hundreds of dhows, often three deep, can be seen tied up along wharfs on the Dubai Creek close to the central business district area, loading all sorts of cargo—from refrigerators to car parts, tyres and food products. Large trucks can be seen on the wharf, full of containers whose contents are then divided and loaded onto the dhows manually by subcontinent expatriates.

Dubai styles itself as the Hong Kong or Singapore of the Gulf. Like Hong Kong and Singapore, many products landing in Dubai are re-exported. Like Hong Kong and Singapore also, Dubai is a city of high-rise office blocks, hotels and apartments. Its tallest buildings include the seven-star luxury hotel, the Burj al Arab, and the Emirates Towers' office and hotel complex. Unlike Hong Kong or Singapore, there is not the same spirit of free trade or competition as many major UAE corporations are government owned or controlled and there are many restrictions placed on foreign residents and companies.

Modern refrigerators and old car parts wait to be loaded onto a dhow on the Dubai Creek for re-export.

To many visitors, dhows tied up in the Dubai Creek represent the most visible sign of foreign trade. However, the real volume of imports, exports and re-exports pass through the container terminals at Port Rashid, near the fashionable upmarket residential district of Jumeriah, and further down the coast to Abu Dhabi at the largest man-made port complex, Jebel Ali.

If You Want to Export Beer, See the Doctor
The UAE does not have uniform import regulations for some commodities. An interesting requirement for the importation of beer into the Emirate of Abu Dhabi is that a medical practitioner in the exporting country needs to certify that the beer is suitable for human consumption.

The UAE does not subsidise exports and re-exports, directly or indirectly.

The Problem of Parallel Imports
Smuggling has long been a tradition of the pirate coast. Parallel imports are goods that enter a country unofficially without going through customs or official distribution channels. Ports in the northern emirates are often used by unofficial distributors to parallel import well known products for sale at a lower price. Unofficial parallel importing disrupts the relationship with appointed distributors, and also makes it difficult to formulate and implement marketing and distribution strategies.

The manufacturer of a leading international brand of beer had difficulty measuring its market penetration. The product was imported from the Netherlands via the appointed distributor as well as through unofficial channels from Singapore.

A Stable Currency
The currency of the UAE, the dirham (UAD) is relatively new, only coming into circulation in 1973. Prior to 1973, UAE's currency was the Bahrain dinar, the Qatar riyal and the Dubai riyal.

The dirham is stable and has been pegged to the US dollar (USD) since 1998 at an exchange rate of UAD 3.67 to USD 1.

There are no currency controls regarding the transfer of funds into or out of the UAE, except that the currency of Israel may not be traded. All other currencies can be traded at market prices and no licence is required to change money. The dirham, made up from 100 fils and bank notes in denominations of 1000, 500, 200, 100, 50, 20 and 5, is freely convertible.

Like the EU and the Euro, the AGCC has, on its financial agenda, a common currency for the region.

Sophisticated Banking and Finance

Bahrain has historically been the financial centre for the Gulf and still has significant offshore banking units. Abu Dhabi is unquestionably the centre for banking and finance in the UAE. The banking and finance system is based on British standards. The Arab Monetary Fund (the Arab world equivalent of the International Monetary Fund) is headquartered in Abu Dhabi as is the Arab Bank for Investment and Foreign Trade (partly owned by the Abu Dhabi government.)

In 1980, a central bank was established replacing the UAE Currency Board created in 1973. The Central Bank's role is to manage credit policy, ensure economic growth, issue currency and regulate the banking and financial sector. As a result of the bad debt crisis in the 1980s occasioned by the collapse of the Bank of Credit Commerce International (BCCI), the Central Bank has been more assertive in regulating the lending provisions of the commercial banks. Regulations introduced in the early 80s by the Central Bank restricted commercial banks to lending no more than 7% of their capital base to an individual or company and no more than 25% to a government agency or public organisation. The Central Bank also required the commercial banks to establish a capital adequacy ratio of 10%.

In the 1970s, a number of foreign banks opened offices in the UAE. By 2001, the central bank had issued 27 licences to foreign banks. Foreign banks can only have a maximum of eight branches in the UAE. The Central Bank is concerned about the number of banks in the UAE and is active in discreetly encouraging weaker banks to merge or be acquired. Should commercial banks become insolvent because of poor lending policies, the Central Bank has measures to ensure that depositors do not lose their funds.

UAE national banks dominate the market. The market is over serviced with approximately 20 UAE incorporated banks having 243 branches and 41 cash offices and a number of specialist banks. The Emirate Industrial Bank specialises in providing loans to new and expanding businesses. Its soft loans have been a catalyst in stimulating growth in the re-export, construction and capital intensive gas industries.

Outside the banking sector, the share of non bank finance to GDP has more than doubled. Non bank finance share of GDP grew from 5.6% in 1980 to 11.5 % in 2000.

Non banking institutions include the Abu Dhabi Investment Authority (with reserves estimated to be USD200 billion in 1999) which focuses on development projects.

Other financial institutions include currency exchange houses. They can range in size from a moneychanger in the souq (market) to institutions transacting hundreds of millions of dirhams per year.

The Abu Dhabi Fund for Development (ADFD) was formed in 1971. Around one third of ADFD funds have been applied to the UAE to upgrade infrastructure, generate employment and improve health and education. The ADFD also provides financial assistance to approximately 50 developing countries.

In the area of e-commerce, the UAE plans to set up an internet based central financial forwarding and clearance facility known as the Payment Gateway System (PGS). The development of the PGS is a joint venture between the business sector and the government.

The UAE was the last AGCC country to have a formal stock exchange. In 2000, the stock exchange, with more than fifty listed stocks, was opened in Abu Dhabi with a link to a trading floor in Dubai. The regulatory authority, the Securities and Commodities Commission based in Abu Dhabi, has the power to license trading floors. Share trading is conducted electronically. There are more than fifty brokerage houses to facilitate the buying and selling of shares. The split stock exchange is symptomatic of the political and economic rivalry that exists between Abu Dhabi and Dubai. UAE stock market indexes include the Nbad and Emnex.

There are plans to open a second stock exchange in Abu Dhabi which would trade exclusively in foreign stocks and be located on Saadiyat Island. Now at the drawing board stage, there are also plans to designate the island as a free trade zone.

A Low/No Taxation Regime

UAE national business enterprises are not taxed on profits and there is no restriction on profit transfer or capital repatriation. Employees do not pay income tax and there are no restrictions on expatriate employees wishing to transfer their salaries to other countries.

Duties and tariffs are generally harmonised throughout the UAE. There are plans to have them harmonised throughout the AGCC countries as well. In 1994, the federal government introduced a 4% tariff on most imports Some products, such as alcoholic beverages, attract higher tariffs. The tariffs only apply to products actually entering the UAE. Goods for re-export are exempt from tax. There are many exemptions. For example, there is no import duty on machinery or raw materials as long as the company is registered with the Industrial Department. There are restrictions on who is allowed to import.

Each emirate raises revenue through taxes or administrative charges. These taxes and charges are paid by businesses and householders to the emirate governments or an agency of the emirate government. The Emirates of Abu Dhabi, Dubai and Sharjah levy a royalty on oil extraction and a small tax on business banking transactions. At the moment, the federal government does not impose any tax in the UAE.

There are also quasi taxes. All businesses must belong to the chamber of commerce of the emirate where they are based. Fees paid to the emirate's chamber of commerce are a quasi tax. Other indirect taxes include fees associated with the business licence (usually paid each year) and transaction fees associated with functions such as the issuing of certificates of origin.

Although direct tax is minimal and indirect tax is modest, additional taxes are levied that are not paid in most countries. One such tax is on rent. In the Emirate of Dubai, there is a municipal tax of 10% on leases paid on commercial property and a 5% tax on leases paid for renting residential property. By global standards, rents for commercial property and residential property are high. As only UAE nationals can own land, rent is an unavoidable business cost.

The biggest hidden overhead expense for overseas business is in paying part of its profits to the UAE partner who usually owns 51% of the business but puts in little effort in the running of the business. The UAE partner is generally referred to as the "sponsor".

There are no taxes and tariffs on inter-emirate transactions.

Expatriates enjoy few of the welfare benefits offered by the government to UAE nationals, and receive and expect little in the way of government services. However, as the burden of indirect taxes increasingly falls on them, they are becoming more critical of the value of government services that they receive.

A Net Creditor Country

The UAE is a net creditor country. As a nation, it does not publish its financial position. In fact the distinction between private and public wealth is somewhat blurred. The rulers of the individual emirates hold foreign investments in their own name as well as in the name of the federation. The amount of foreign holdings can only be estimated, but is thought to be in the region of USD 100 billion. In the 1990s, the level of foreign debt was about USD 11 billion—making the UAE a net creditor country of about USD 90 billion. Most of this debt comprise short-term liabilities to finance trade and development projects. It is estimated that more than 95% of foreign debt is owed to commercial creditors and 5% is government debt. The UAE is a capital exporting country.

Individual emirates also lend to, and borrow from, the world on their own accounts. For example, according to the IMF, the Abu Dhabi Investment Authority has foreign investments in stocks and bonds to the value of USD 80 billion. It is also believed that foreign assets owned by the Emirate of Dubai are greater than the foreign assets owned by the federal government.

In the area of public expenditure, the federal budget represented only 50% with the other 50% coming from individual emirates, and Abu Dhabi and Dubai in particular.

Disparity of Income

Although per capita GDP for the UAE is high by global standards at USD 17,240 in 1995, it ranges from USD 32,066 for Abu Dhabi to USD 6,311 for Ajman.

An Economy of Foreign Workers

Since the discovery of oil in the mid 1950s, the UAE has been dependent on expatriates to manage and work in their enterprises. Foreigners and male expatriates, in particular, still dominate the work force. Most of the foreign workers in the UAE remit a large part of their income home.

Foreign workers can be categorized into three main groups. The first group comprises western expatriates who are mainly from First World countries. They make up 5% to 10% of the work force. Most western expatriates obtain a job in the UAE through networking, transfers or job advertisements in newspapers and business magazines. Along with the rest of the world, UAE companies use the internet to source candidates.

The second group comprises subcontinent expatriates, broadly defined as expatriates mainly from Afghanistan, Bangladesh, India, Pakistan and Sri Lanka. They make up the vast majority of blue collar workers. No one, except AGCC and British nationals, may enter the UAE unless they are sponsored by a UAE national or a UAE company. Most subcontinent expatriates are sponsored either by their employers or individuals who are UAE nationals. Where subcontinent expatriates are sponsored by an individual UAE national, it is the management of the company and not the sponsor who will find accommodation for the expatriate workers. Most unskilled subcontinent expatriates are accommodated in labour camps with fairly rudimentary facilities. This can lead to abuse. There have been reports in the press by some employees, working as builders and labourers in the construction industry, that they are not issued with basic safety equipment such as helmets, gloves and safety boots.

In a move to improve conditions for blue collar expatriates, the Crown Prince of Dubai has issued an order banning the transportation of workers in open trucks or pickups. The Abu Dhabi government has also warned companies to use a suitable form of transport for their workers. Trucks are allowed as long as the cargo area is covered and there are proper seating arrangements.

The third group of expatriates come from Asia— mainly from China, Japan, Korea, the Philippines and Singapore. It is the only group with a significant number of female workers. Filipinos make up a significant proportion of those employed in the hotels or as domestic help to UAE nationals or expatriate managers. A recent trend has seen an increase in the number of expatriates recruited from China to work in the hotel industry. Asian expatriates make up approximately 10% of the work force.

There is a fourth group of overseas workers who are not generally referred to as expatriates. They are non Gulf Arabs from Egypt, Lebanon, Palestine and Syria who make up between 5% and 10% of the work force.

Each category of expatriates used to work in fairly clearly defined occupations. For example, western expatriates used to fill most of the senior management roles while subcontinent expatriates used to fill most of the tradesmen or technician positions. This is changing. Today, many senior divisional general managers in major UAE corporations are subcontinent expatriates; more western expatriates can be found in less senior positions as well as in the service sector, for example, as waiters in theme outlets such as an Irish pub.

Labour contracts for all expatriates are normally for one year but can be renewed. Most western expatriates spend a relatively short period of their career in the UAE whereas subcontinent expatriates can spend nearly their whole career in the UAE, working 20 years or more in the same company on a series of consecutive one-year contracts. When they retire, expatriates cannot stay in the UAE; they can never become citizens of the UAE nor can they own land.

The government is able to regulate the number of foreign workers in the country through the issue of work visas. To apply for a work visa for an employee, an employer must demonstrate to the government that a genuine job vacancy exists so that in theory, the demand for foreign labour matches the supply. In practice, there are short-term shortages and excesses not helped by subcontinent expatriates who enter the UAE without the correct documentation and become illegal workers. A method used by expatriates, mainly from the subcontinent, to illegally obtain work in the UAE, is to enter on a tourist visa and not leave when their visa expires.

Living conditions for illegal workers are fairly primitive and accommodation is squalid. Most illegal workers are single. They earn less than their legal counterparts, but more than what they would in their home country.

In 1996, as a result of a large build up of illegal foreign workers, the government offered an amnesty to allow them to leave the country with few penalties. Some 200,000 illegal workers took advantage of the offer, causing labour shortages in the UAE, particularly in the construction industry. The construction industry also experienced cost increases because the illegal workers had been paid lower wages. Employers had to bear higher employee overheads as there was no government ratified labour contract.

The so-called Russian problem emerged in 1998, with CIS citizens, including a thousand or so prostitutes, headed for Dubai as tourists. The sight of prostitutes in hotels began to tarnish the image of Dubai as a tourist destination, and the Crown Prince issued an order banning visitor visas for single, unaccompanied women.

In 1999, there was another surplus of unskilled workers and UAE diplomatic missions were advised not to issue visas to unskilled workers from the subcontinent. Ras al Khaimah became a favoured port of entry for illegal workers because it had a number of businesses, holding tourist licences, that were willing to sponsor illegal workers as tourists. To stop the problem, the Government of Ras al Khaimah refused to renew tourist licenses and substantially increased the fine for businesses with tourist licences that brought in bogus tourists.

The Emirate of Abu Dhabi has also been active in rounding up illegal workers. The concern has also been that illegal workers destabilise the demographic balance of the population and represent a security threat. The government is particularly concerned about radical Muslim groups and, in particular, workers from Bangladesh and Pakistan. The security forces and the police keep close surveillance on the expatriate community and do not tolerate any political activity or tension amongst groups of foreign workers.

Keeping a balance of the large foreign work force is always a problem for the government and it addresses the issue in a pragmatic way. For example, this is seen in the change in rules for the removal of illegal visitors. The old regulations stipulated that expatriates caught staying in the UAE illegally had to first serve a two-month jail sentence before being deported. In 2001, the two-month jail sentence was scrapped because of overcrowding at Taweelah prison where illegal visitors had been detained. Up to 2,000 illegal visitors are deported each month.

A recent innovation is the issue of high-tech labour cards by the government which would keep a better surveillance on foreign workers.

UAE Nationals as a Minority in the UAE

UAE nationals, who only account for one quarter to one third of the population, enjoy one of the world's highest per capita income and a welfare system equal to anywhere in the world. The rulers of the emirates are strong advocates for the redistribution of wealth amongst UAE nationals as a means of securing loyalty.

In 2001, UAE nationals made up approximately one third of the work force. It is the objective of the government to have UAE nationals make up at least half the work force. Companies are required to give preference, when recruiting, to UAE nationals.

In Abu Dhabi, the government has instructed foreign companies operating in the construction and oil industry to reserve a specific number of jobs for UAE nationals. The problem is the shortage of UAE nationals with managerial and technical skills. To address this issue, the National Authority for Employment and Human Resource Management is working with companies to provide on-the-job training.

Some organisations, such as the Dubai Ports and Customs Service, have developed an automatic enquiry service to handle job applications from UAE nationals. Other companies have outsourced their human resource function.

Although companies are required to give preference to UAE nationals, many small to medium-sized companies and limited liability companies find a way around this requirement because UAE nationals cost a lot more to employ. The few UAE nationals who work in the private sector earn significantly more than their subcontinent counterparts. Starting salaries for graduates who are UAE nationals were around UAD 8,000 per month in 2001. Even high school leavers were paid UAD 5,000 per month. This compares to salaries of approximately UAD 4,000 per month paid to subcontinent expatriate graduates with relevant job experience.

On top of this, private sector employers are obliged to pay 12.5% of the salary of a UAE national into a superannuation fund.

As a result of having to pay higher salaries to UAE nationals, newspapers reported in 2001 that there were over 500 UAE graduates unemployed despite there being many vacancies.

Government Decree to Increase Employment of UAE Nationals
Cabinet decree #10, issued in 1998, requires banks to increase the employment of UAE nationals at a rate of 4% per annum. The Central Bank is empowered to penalize commercial banks who do not achieve their 4% growth target.

How the UAE Government is to be Emiratised
The UAE government, in 2001, created a new human resource development and employment authority—Tanmia. The plan is for Tanmia to train and recruit 3,000 UAE nationals per year for the UAE civil service and the private sector. To ensure that UAE nationals obtain jobs in government, there are plans to ban the recruitment of expatriates in certain occupations. So far, the greatest number of candidates in the programme have come from women in Dubai.

Although there is considerable media coverage about the need for companies to increase the number of UAE nationals in their employ, senior members of the business community who are UAE nationals say that the country will always need an international work force. In fact, many UAE nationals, who are senior figures in the business community, attribute the UAE's economic success to its international work force.

UAE nationals are selective in the jobs that they take, preferring to be federal civil servants. In 2001, they made up nearly half the work force in this sector. Somewhat interestingly, UAE nationals have an aversion to working in local governments where they made up less than a fifth of the work force in 2001. Ironically, UAE nationals do not have the skills nor do they like to work in the oil fields (a significant contributor to their wealth) where they make up less than 10% of the work force. UAE nationals are averse to taking on *blue collar* jobs, jobs of low prestige and jobs such as commissioned salesmen where remuneration is based on performance. These jobs are filled by non Gulf Arabs and subcontinent expatriates. In view of this situation, the government may grant some long term expatriates permanent residency to ensure the continued growth of the economy and to provide competition to UAE national workers. In the future, expatriate workers may be granted privileges such as the right to own land.

The authors, on their recent visit to the UAE, were surprised to learn that about a quarter of the students at one of the higher colleges of technology required a loan to purchase a relatively low cost personal computer. When questioned, one member of the academic staff informed us that there is a small group of relatively poor UAE nationals who are seeking to advance themselves in society by self-education and working in professions.

The population of the UAE is skewed towards male expatriates mainly from the subcontinent and this is likely to remain so in the medium term. In the longer term, as the economy diversifies and becomes less dependent on oil and as many state-owned enterprises become privatised, there will be greater pressure for UAE nationals to obtain real jobs, thus reducing the proportion of expatriates in the work force. With the tightening labour market and fewer *white collar* employment opportunities available, UAE nationals may have to work in less glamorous occupations such as on farms and as agricultural labourers.

Another new employment avenue for UAE nationals who graduate from the Higher Colleges of Education is to work in the travel industry as tour guides. A few recently graduated UAE nationals have taken up positions with major international companies like Coca Cola in junior management positions such as an Assistant Brand Manager.

The government is hopeful that with the opening of new technology parks like Dubai Media City, there will be new employment opportunities for UAE nationals in the media and related fields.

UAE nationals do not have much of a say in evolving strategy for the economy. In 2001, less than 1% of UAE nationals had a role in this area.

More Emiratis for Emirates

The Emirates Group is best known for its high profile affiliate, Emirates Airlines. In 1999, only 550 of the 12,000 employees were UAE nationals. To redress the poor representation of UAE nationals, Emirates Airlines plans to recruit and train more UAE nationals each year. The company has established the National Recruitment and Development Centre with an objective in 2001 to recruit 200 of the most talented UAE Nationals. Emirates have also been active in developing UAE executives to take up more senior appointments. In 2001, three UAE nationals were promoted to senior management positions in the areas of logistics, marketing and general management.

> **Etisalat Employs More Emiratis**
> In 1998, only 28% of employees of Emirates Telecommunications Corporation (Etisalat) were UAE nationals. Etisalat has a substantial budget to develop a training programme with the objective of making half their work force, UAE nationals by 2002.
>
> Some western expatriate lecturers at the Higher Colleges of Education have expressed a concern that their graduates have unrealistic employment expectations. Many UAE nationals who graduate expect fast track promotion despite their ability. Another criticism is that UAE nationals tend to take more time off and are less committed to the objectives of their organisation than their other colleagues.

Unlike in many First World countries where government salaries lag behind private sector salaries, the reverse is true in the UAE. Salaries and conditions of work for UAE nationals in the federal civil service and the civil service of Abu Dhabi compare very favourably to the private sector.

In December 1996, Abu Dhabi raised government salaries by 20% making the gap between the income of UAE nationals and expatriates even wider. The two biggest employers in the UAE are the government and the business sector. The majority of small trading businesses are 100% owned and operated by UAE nationals. Larger businesses tend to be operated in partnership with foreign businesses.

Increased Competition from Bahrain

Bahrain may re-emerge as a competitor to Dubai for companies to locate their regional offices. It is in the process of liberalising its commercial laws to allow companies to operate without a sponsor as is required in the UAE. Also, as part of its commercial liberalisation, is a plan to allow foreign companies and individuals to own land. In 1999, Bahrain allowed AGCC citizens to own real estate. In a further liberalisation, the Amir of Bahrain decreed that foreign-owned companies operating in the areas of trade, tourism, industry, banking and finance can own land and buildings. Newspaper reports suggest that the liberalisation is calculated to restore Bahrain as the financial and banking hub of the Gulf. The UAE currently allows foreigners to purchase houses in selected areas but not ownership of land.

Bahrain also has the advantage of a lower cost of operations for companies when compared to Abu Dhabi and Dubai. This is because the cost of leasing business premises, housing for expatriate management employees and expatriate salaries are lower in Bahrain than the UAE. In addition, Bahrainis work at all levels in businesses. Expatriates from the UAE are often surprised that the taxi drivers are actually Bahrainis. Bahrain is the home in the Gulf for offshore banking units (OBUs). The UAE could have persuaded more OBUs to relocate from Bahrain to Abu Dhabi and Dubai but did not do so for political reasons. Slightly more than half of Bahrain's population are Shi'ite Muslims but the ruling family and the minority of the population are Sunni Muslims. Iran, whose population is mostly Shi'ite Muslims, has territorial claim on Bahrain and some islands off the coast of the UAE.

The UAE was, and still is, concerned that if it economically weakened Bahrain there could be renewed political initiatives for Iran to claim Bahrain and as part of that initiative, the islands off the coast of the UAE may become an issue. So for political, rather than strictly commercial, reasons Bahrain remains competitive to the UAE as a regional centre.

CHAPTER 3

The Government

Overview

Up until 1996, the UAE operated a provisional constitution which was reviewed every five years. This reflected the fragile nature of the federation. In 1996, the emirates agreed to make the constitution permanent, recognising Abu Dhabi as the national capital and the centre for political leadership.

The style of government and political leadership in the emirates can best be described as a benevolent dictatorship. A shaikh or "emir" (meaning prince) rule each emirate. It is a hereditary position. In the past, the people belonged to one of seven tribes. Each tribe elected a shaikh who heads the tribe. Unlike western democracies, there is no organised or official pan-emirate opposition.

The benevolence of the shaikhs is displayed in a number of ways, including the release of prisoners at Ramadan. The ruler of Abu Dhabi, who is also the president of the UAE, displays his benevolence by visiting the souq on a regular basis and buying from each shop whether he needs the merchandise or not. To encourage citizens to invest in the country, the shaikhs invest in businesses in the UAE.

The UAE has three levels of government: the federal government, the emirate governments (seven, one for each emirate) and the municipal or regional governments. Although the federal government is the highest authority, the emirate government is the most powerful level of government. Each emirate has its own civil service managing civil aviation, oil, internal security, finance and economic policy.

The federal government is responsible for foreign affairs, defence, nationality and immigration issues, education, public health, postal, telephone and other communication services, air traffic control, licensing of aircraft, labour relations, banking, and the determination of territorial waters.

Lack of a Federal Vision

It is a moot point as to how united the emirates are. There has been considerable competition between the rulers of the emirates, and specifically between the ruling families of Abu Dhabi and Dubai. In the emirate government, the ruler is the head of state and head of government. Both positions are hereditary. As Abu Dhabi and Dubai make the most contributions to the UAE government's coffers, they hold most of the important cabinet posts. The ruler of Abu Dhabi, the largest emirate and the wealthiest by far, is always the president of the UAE. The ruler of Dubai, the next wealthiest emirate, is always the deputy president of the federation—the most senior position after the president. The ruler of Dubai is also usually the prime minister of the federation. Federal ministers are appointed from all the emirates, with Abu Dhabi holding the greatest number of portfolios.

The federal government and the emirate governments have focused on reducing the country's dependence on oil but a lack of co-ordinated planning exists because the rulers of the emirates are reluctant to give up their own power to the federal government. This has led to duplication and over-capacity in areas of the economy such as infrastructure, and underdevelopment in others.

UAE nationals identify themselves first as a citizen of their emirate, and then as a citizen of the UAE just as some Americans identify themselves first as Californians, but this is changing. Younger UAE nationals, many born after the federation, are starting to refer to themselves as *emiratis* in the same way that people from Bahrain refer to themselves as Bahrainis and people from Kuwait refer to themselves as Kuwaitis.

The authors found it curious that when interviewing business people on topics such as the economy, the interviewee would give

The love the people have for Shaikh Zayed, the president of the UAE and the ruler of Abu Dhabi, is clearly shown by this picture of him draped from the building.

a detailed account of their emirate (for example, Dubai) but not a picture of the national economy.

A symbolic reflection of the parochial nature of the UAE is the non availability of telephone books. You will only find the Abu Dhabi telephone book in Abu Dhabi, the Dubai telephone book in Dubai and the Sharjah telephone book in Sharjah. In most countries, state or provincial telephone books are easily accessible.

Although there does not seem to be an articulated strategic vision for the UAE, Dubai certainly has one. Shaikh Maktoum, vice president of the UAE and ruler of Dubai, has stated that, "Our strategic vision for Dubai is to be the centre of excellence not only for West Asia, but the rest of the world."

Supreme Council of Rulers

The top policy making body is the Supreme Council of Rulers. Its members are the rulers of the seven emirates. Theoretically, the Supreme Council of Rulers decides on policies and elects the federal president and vice president for five-year terms—a mere formality since the president is always the ruler of Abu Dhabi and the vice president is the ruler of Dubai. It also admits new members to the federation, appoints and dismisses the prime minister and judges of the Federal Supreme Court and ratifies federal laws. The president of the UAE appoints the prime minister and cabinet, and has the power to amend federal laws.

In reality, the ruling families of Abu Dhabi and Dubai have a big say in these decisions because of their economic importance to the federation. It is no coincidence that the president of the UAE is always the ruler of Abu Dhabi, and the vice president is always the ruler of Dubai, as well as, usually, the prime minister.

The Council of Ministers

This is the second most important body after the Supreme Council. Council members from Abu Dhabi and Dubai and, to a lesser extent, Sharjah hold the most important ministerial portfolios. The role of the Council of Ministers is to initiate legislation ratified by the Supreme Council of Rulers, approve the federal budget and oversee the federal government. Approximately one quarter of the cabinet is associated with the Abu Dhabi royal family, again reinforcing Abu Dhabi's importance to the federation. Cabinet usually meets every week. The prime minister chairs cabinet meetings and in his absence, the deputy prime minister, who is also a member of the Abu Dhabi royal family.

Federal National Council

The Federal National Council is the legislative body but its role is more consultative than legislative. The president of the UAE, in consultation with the rulers of the emirates, appoints the 40-member council.

Theoretically, these numbers reflect the population size, but in reality, they reflect the political and economic clout of each emirate. Abu Dhabi and Dubai each sends eight members, Ras al Khaimah and Sharjah each sends six members, and Ajman, Fujairah and Umm al Qaiwain each sends four members. Members are appointed for two-year terms.

The Federal National Council deals with issues that include the freedom of the press as well as the building and development of a national culture. They are particularly fond of praising the leadership of their benefactor—the president of the UAE and the ruler of Abu Dhabi.

The Federal Judiciary

There are three levels in the federal court system: the federal Supreme Court, the Courts of First Instance, and the Appellate Courts. The president of the UAE appoints the federal Supreme Court judges with the approval of the Supreme Council of Rulers. The federal Supreme Court consists of a chairman and up to five judges. The court, which only sits if formally requested, deals with constitutional matters, inter-emirate disputes and disputes between the federal government and the emirate governments, and very serious crimes against the federation. Very occasionally will the Supreme Court hear a commercial case. In a landmark decision in 1992 relating to a commercial case, the court held that a foreign arbitration clause in a registered commercial agency agreement was unenforceable as a matter of public policy.

The Courts of First Instance deal with civil, commercial, criminal and personal disputes.

Whereas there is a culture of litigation in the west and in the United States, in particular, this is best avoided in the UAE. The major objective in hiring a lawyer in the UAE is to put arrangements in place so that there will be no need to litigate if there is a dispute. Litigation can be long and drawn-out and outcomes often favour UAE nationals. Hearings in the courts are in Arabic and, in most instances, only lawyers who are UAE nationals can appear. UAE law is based on Egyptian law which is French-based. There are a number of Australian, British and other foreign legal firms practising in the UAE which can advise on commercial matters including how best to set up your company.

Don't Rely Too Much on the Law

A British company in the oil exploration business had one of its vehicles involved in an accident with a vehicle owned and driven by a UAE national. As is the custom in the UAE, the police attended to the matter before the vehicles were towed away, and identified the UAE national as the cause of the accident. It was mutually agreed amongst all parties that the UAE national would pay the cost of repairs. Unfortunately, the UAE national had no insurance and could not pay. In a surprise move, he brought an action in the courts against the oil exploration company for damages to *his* vehicle. Although the UAE national was unsuccessful in his counter claim, the oil exploration company was also not compensated for the damage to the company vehicle as there was no enforcement of the court decision.

Complementing the Supreme Court and Courts of First Instance are the emirate-based *Shariah* Courts. They administer Islamic law within the legal system of each emirate. The Shariah Courts deal with breaches of religious law, matters which involve *diya* or blood money and moral crimes. They can hand out brutal punishments. The Fujairah Shariah Court sentenced three UAE nationals and six subcontinent expatriates to jail sentences of more than one year plus a hundred lashes for adultery. Four of the accused were women.

> **What Life is Worth in the UAE**
> In a recent case, the Shariah Court in Abu Dhabi awarded the brother-in-law of two relatives killed in a car accident, the sum of UAD 150,000 for each relative who died in the accident, as diya or blood money. In addition, the brother-in-law had the right to claim further compensation in a civil court.

Stable Politics

By Middle East standards, the UAE offers a relatively stable political and economic environment. It is a member of the United Nations, the Arab League and the AGCC. The AGCC, although chiefly concerned with economic issues, includes security and defence matters in its agenda.

In 1991, the UAE contributed approximately USD 10 billion to assist coalition military forces expel Iraq's army from Kuwait. In 1996, the UAE signed a loose defence agreement with the US.

Regional issues include an unresolved dispute with Iran over the ownership of the islands of Abu Musa and Greater and Lesser Tunb. Iran occupied Greater and Lesser Tunb islands in 1971 and, in 1992, took full control of Abu Musa Island which it had shared with Sharjah since 1971. In 1995, the UAE openly criticised Iran for the occupation of the three islands. What is at stake is ownership of the oil fields lying beneath these tiny islands. The dispute is likely to remain deadlocked for the immediate future.

To maintain regional stability, the UAE has made substantial donations to more than 30 development projects in 13 Arab countries. Donors have included the federal government, the emirate governments, the rulers of the emirates and private citizens.

Internally, the UAE is concerned about Islamic militancy and the political activities of the expatriate work force. It is pragmatic about political issues, and, like Egypt, it seeks to resolve political problems with commercial solutions. The UAE is largely unaffected by political ideologies although it does support the Arab boycott of Israel.

When the Ruler Attends the Dubai Cup
The Dubai Cup is a major international horse racing event and an important social one that the ruler of Dubai attends. Although the UAE is politically stable, great security measures are taken when the ruler appears in public. These include keeping secret his exact time of arrival. The motorcade will consist of three identical, black, stretched Mercedes Benz with curtains drawn. Nobody knows which limousine the ruler travels in. A helicopter from the UAE armed forces will hover overhead in case of trouble.

The Majlis
The *majlis* is the nearest equivalent in the UAE of western democracy. Traditionally, the *majlis* was a meeting where common people bearing a grievance could petition the ruler. The *majilis* provides the ruler with an opportunity to know the people's thoughts. Theoretically, any leading member of UAE society can hold a *majlis*. In practice, the ruler of an emirate or a member of the royal family holds it. Attendees at the *majlis* sometimes request financial assistance for a sick child needing medical treatment overseas, from the ruler. More recently, unemployed UAE nationals seek help to look for a job.

Emirate of Abu Dhabi

The Royal Family

There is genuine affection by all UAE nationals for the ruler of Abu Dhabi, Shaikh Zayed, who is also the president of the UAE and a symbol of unity for the federation. When he returned in 2001 from an operation in the US, welcoming banners and pictures of the ruler were everywhere—along the main roads, at the airports and major shopping and business centres—wishing him a speedy recovery. Pictures of the president of the UAE and the ruler of Abu Dhabi are almost mandatory in government and business offices throughout the UAE to remind people of the importance of the federation and of Shaikh Zayed as a symbol of unity.

Members of the royal family play a key role in the government of the UAE. The Crown Prince of Abu Dhabi, Khalifa bin Zayed al Nahayan, is the Deputy Supreme Commander of the UAE Armed Forces and Chairman of the Executive Council of the Emirate of Abu Dhabi. Who will succeed the Crown Prince is not so clear cut. The Crown Prince has a different mother from the ruler's other sons. There is speculation that Shaikh Mohammed, one of the sons of Bani Fatima, the ruler's favourite wife, may be the next Crown Prince.

The executive council, chaired by the Crown Prince, is the cabinet of the Emirate of Abu Dhabi.

National Consultative Council

In accordance with the principle of *shura* (or consultation), the ruler of Abu Dhabi formed the emirate's National Consultative Council in 1970. The 55 members of the National Consultative Council are heads of the main tribes and families in the Emirate of Abu Dhabi. The ruler appoints members to the council. The chairman of the council is known as the speaker, giving the Emirate of Abu Dhabi a veneer of parliament.

Members serve a two-year term and the council sits for eight months of the year usually commencing in November. One of the NCC roles is to receive petitions and complaints from citizens.

Within the Emirate of Abu Dhabi there are four regions and two municipalities. The Abu Dhabi region includes the city of Abu Dhabi, which is also the federal capital, and Abu Dhabi island.

The eastern region centres on Al Ain city, home of the UAE's first university. The head of the regional administration is known as the Ruler's Representative.

The capital of the western region is Bida Zayed, also known as Zayed City. The region comprises 52 villages. Like the eastern region, the head of the regional administration has the title, Ruler's Representative.

Das Island, best known for its important oil and gas terminal, is also an administrative region. It is also headed by a Ruler's Representative.

The cities of Abu Dhabi and Al Ain each have an appointed municipal council.

Emirate of Dubai

As with Abu Dhabi, the royal family of Dubai has considerable influence in the UAE. The ruler of Dubai, Shaikh Maktoum, is also the vice president and prime minister of the UAE. In 1994, Mohammed bin Rashed al Maktoum, his younger brother, was appointed Crown Prince. Shaikh Mohammed is a general in the UAE Armed Forces and also the Minister for Defence in the federal cabinet. He is reputed to be one of the most powerful figures in the UAE and has a high media profile. He is effectively the ruler of Dubai and is expected to succeed the current ruler of Dubai. Another prominent member of the Dubai royal family is the Deputy Ruler of Dubai. He is Minister for Finance and Industry in the federal cabinet, reflecting the importance of Dubai as the commercial capital of the UAE.

> **Efficiency in the Civil Service**
> On a morning visit to a number of government offices, the Crown Prince of Dubai was surprised to find only a few heads of departments in, although office hours were from 8:30 a.m. He summarily fired all heads of department who had not shown up for work that day. He then decreed that all heads of department should report to the palace each day at 10:00 a.m. to report on their department's activities. Since this incident, government heads and their senior personnel have used the early morning hours to prepare their daily reports and there is little point in making appointments with senior government officials in Dubai until about 12 noon.

In other measures to improve government efficiency, the Crown Prince has streamlined waiting time at government counters and ordered the removal of glass partitions to make civil servants appear friendlier.

Emirate of Sharjah
In addition to the ruler of Sharjah, two other members of the royal family are deputy rulers of the Emirate of Sharjah. Kalba and Khor Fakkan are administrative regions which are headed by a deputy chairman each.

Emirate of Ras al Khaimah
In addition to the ruler, Ras Al Khaimah has two deputy rulers who are members of the royal family.

Emirate of Ajman
Ajman has a ruler and a deputy ruler who is the Crown Prince.

Emirate of Fujairah
Fujairah has a ruler and a deputy ruler who is not the crown prince.

Emirate of Umm al Qaiwain
Umm al Qaiwain has a ruler and the crown prince serves as a deputy ruler.

Emirs and Walis
Smaller and more remote areas have emirs or walis, who are appointed by the rulers of the emirates to interface between the people and the royal family.

Business and the Bureaucracy
The UAE civil service is modelled after the British civil service. What is particularly frustrating to expatriates doing business in the UAE is that each emirate maintains its own government and civil service in addition to the federal bureaucracy. There is no federal customs and numerous documents are required to support an application for a government permit or licence. This can take some time as numerous documents are shuffled from one civil servant to another. Red tape is another feature of dealing with the various civil service departments. One exception is the highly efficient Dubai Customs Service where documentation can be lodged electronically.

Emirate bureaucracies vary in size, with Abu Dhabi and Dubai having substantial economic and public works departments. In the smaller emirates, the bureaucracy is an extension of the office of the ruler. Differences exist in the efficiency levels of the various emirate governments. Businesses usually find it harder to work with the Abu Dhabi and Sharjah government departments and easier with government departments in Dubai. This could be due to the fact that Abu Dhabi and Sharjah civil servants do not have the same international business acumen that Dubai civil servants have. One difficulty in dealing with the junior and middle ranking civil service officers in Abu Dhabi and Sharjah is that they are disorganized and do not have a strong work ethic. Parkinson's first law that work expands to meet the time available is practised by UAE bureaucrats. *"They want everything tomorrow—then sleep on it for months"* was a comment made by a former diplomat, on the efficiency of the federal civil service.

Although most private sector employees are not UAE nationals, the reverse is true in the UAE federal civil service and the emirates' bureaucracy, which almost exclusively employ UAE nationals in the senior ranks. There are, however, many non Gulf Arabs including Egyptians, Lebanese, Palestinians and Syrians who act as advisors to senior civil service officers or who work in middle management or junior management positions in the bureaucracy. The National Authority for Employment and Human Resources has targeted federal ministries, emirate government departments and local government departments as employment opportunities for unemployed graduate UAE nationals.

> **Dealing with the Federal and Emirate Governments**
> A director of a British firm involved in oil exploration had significant dealings with the federal and emirate governments. He believed that, to get things done quickly and efficiently, it was necessary to have someone who could speak gulf Arabic, the dialect spoken by UAE nationals who would generally be in the more senior positions; and classical Arabic, the language spoken by Egyptians, Lebanese, Palestinians and Syrians, and middle and lower ranking officials. It was his view that if you don't have someone who can speak both gulf and classical Arabic, the bureaucracy moved at its own pace, not yours. His solution was to hire a woman Egyptian accountant. She was assertive and able to make the bureaucrats move at her pace.

Expatriates dealing with UAE government officials report that there is not the same degree of time management as in western companies. Often, when an appointment has been made weeks in advance, it needs to be constantly confirmed and reconfirmed.

The purchasing departments of the federal government and the emirate governments give preferential treatment to goods produced in the UAE. In the case of the Emirate of Dubai, under the 1986 Ministerial Decree, number 13, goods produced in the UAE are given a 10% price advantage as long as the company is registered with the Industrial Department and has 51% UAE ownership. The other major condition to qualify for preferential pricing treatment is that the value-added component in the UAE must be not less than 40%. There are also other minor conditions.

Although the UAE government encourages overseas companies to locate in the UAE, it is only on condition that they have a UAE sponsor. The federal government and emirate governments do not give direct financial assistance to business for research and development projects.

For companies who do not actually have an operation in the UAE, their contact with the government will be through the UAE commercial agent who is usually the master distributor responsible for importing and marketing the product in the UAE. Another government issue that can arise for exporters of consumer goods is ingredient labelling, which could be different from the requirements of the home or other export markets.

Government and Business

The UAE government's official policy is pro business. It believes that the private sector is the key to providing full employment to UAE nationals. The UAE government provides excellent government facilities and superior business support services, streamlined administrative procedures, up-to-date commercial laws and a favourable tax regime. A major objective of the UAE government is for the country to become a regional business hub.

The UAE, a member of the World Trade Organisation (WTO) since 1995, has been granted certain exemptions from the charter. It is allowed job discriminations in favour of UAE nationals and exclusive UAE shareholding in selected companies that operate in the financial and service sectors of the economy. The UAE is also a party to the General Agreement on Trade in Services (GATS) and the agreement on trade-related aspects of intellectual property.

Chambers of Commerce with Real Clout

Each emirate in the UAE has its own chamber of commerce. In western countries such as the US or the UK, one of the major roles of the chamber of commerce is to lobby government. In the UAE, the emirate chambers of commerce do not lobby but act as a bridge between government and business. The quasi government tasks that the chambers of commerce perform include the issue of business licences and resolving commercial disputes. Companies operating in the UAE must usually be a member of a chamber of commerce.

The Abu Dhabi Chamber of Commerce and Industry (ADCCI) is one of the principal organisations dealing with business on behalf of the Abu Dhabi government. The ADCCI simplifies matters for foreign businesses wanting to establish operations in Abu Dhabi as they do not need to deal directly with government bureaucrats.

With more than 50,000 members, the ADCCI is the largest chamber of commerce in the AGCC countries. Each year it issues approximately 40,000 business licences. The ADCCI also formulates economic regulations and through the Shaikh Khalifa fund provide technical and financial assistance to small to medium-sized business enterprises (SMEs) developed by younger UAE nationals. The ADCCI is also involved in programmes such as the *passport for work* that trains UAE nationals to work in the private sector.

Other ADCCI activities include staging trade fairs, sending missions abroad to promote Abu Dhabi as a commercial centre and receiving overseas trade delegations. An expanding area of its business is the mounting of exhibitions and trade shows, especially the international military exhibitions known as CODEX and IDEX. Other services provided by the chamber include the development of a data bank on members

The ADCCI also settles commercial disputes. There have been no significant disputes involving foreign companies but contractor disputes do occasionally occur. To speed up the resolution of commercial disputes, the ADCCI has established a Commercial Conciliation and Arbitration Centre to specifically focus on agency agreements with foreign companies.

The ADCCI has two branches—one in Abu Dhabi and the other in Al Ain.

The Dubai Chamber of Commerce and Industry (DCCI) operates on similar lines as the ADCCI and provides statistical data on business opportunities as well as advises its members on new regulations promulgated by the Dubai government. It also publishes magazines, commercial directories and mounts trade shows to stimulate business.

The chamber's quasi government role includes authenticating certificates of origin, attesting to the validity of signatures and providing experts to survey goods. Other quasi government functions include the issue of registration certificates to prove a company's trading capacity.

The Dubai Chamber of Commerce and Industry also holds economic forums and seminars. In commercial disputes, the DCCI has a fairly flexible set of rules that allows its members to choose either conciliation or arbitration.

It furnishes overseas companies interested in doing business in Dubai, with names of chamber members who may be suitable partners, and develops profiles of countries trading with the UAE and Dubai. The chamber also sends delegations overseas and receives overseas delegations and foreign chambers of commerce. It negotiates directly with foreign government departments of trade to participate in events such as the Khartoum International Exhibition.

The chambers of commerce in the UAE are aware of the economy's dependence on oil and have been active in attracting new businesses to diversify from this dependence. Unfortunately, foreign business people have commented that the downside is that officials from the chambers of commerce engage in a lot of talk, are very polite but are not really action orientated to conclude a deal.

CHAPTER 4

Infrastructure

Too Many Modern Ports

The UAE has more ports per capita than probably anywhere else in the world. Each emirate has its own port and some have more than one port.

A number of overseas shippers have commented that Dubai is the most efficient port in the UAE and Abu Dhabi, the least efficient. There is no national seaport authority. Each emirate manages its own ports.

Abu Dhabi The Abu Dhabi Seaports Authority manages ports in the Emirate of Abu Dhabi. These ports include Mina Zayed, the gateway (container) port, the Dhow Harbour Mussafah Port (which has also been developed as a free trade zone), Umm al Nar Port and Ras Sadr Port—which are also harbours for dhows and other smaller craft. Jebel Dhanna is the offshore oil export terminal. ADNOC has two tanker fleets. The Abu Dhabi National Tanker Company has its home port at Jebel Dhanna where oil is physically distributed to global markets. Abu Dhabi's second tanker fleet, the National Gas Shipping Company, has the largest gas carriers in the world and ships liquefied natural gas from its terminal at Das Island.

Mina Zayed is one of smaller ports in the UAE handling approximately 10% of the container throughput in 2001. The port is marketing itself as a hub where goods can be trans-shipped by road to other destinations further up the Gulf where higher shipping insurance rates would otherwise apply.

Dubai The Dubai Port Authority is responsible for Jebel Ali Port, Port Rashid and a number of ports for smaller vessels. Jebel

Ali is the world's largest artificial port with the capacity to store 12,000 containers. It is probably the most active duty free zone in the Middle East. Associated with the port is a fleet of approximately 50 trucks taking containers to other destinations in the UAE and to other AGCC markets including Kuwait, Oman, Qatar and Saudi Arabia. The port of Jebel Ali provides a number of other services including the repair and maintenance of containers.

Port Rashid has 36 berths and specialises in handling containers of different sizes. It operates 24 hours every day and containers can be stored in the 22 transit sheds for up to 35 days before incurring duty.

The third sea port in the Emirate of Dubai is Hamriyah Port. Its role is to receive smaller and medium-sized vessels, mainly dhows, sailing to other ports in the Arabian Gulf, the Indian subcontinent and East Africa. To encourage dhows to continue to visit Port Hamriyah, there are no port fees. Hamriyyah Port has also become an important terminal for the export of liquefied natural gas and condensate from the onshore oil fields in Dubai.

The Port of Dubai and the Australian Military

The Australian government and Australian business sector have long been concerned about the low level of productivity on Australian wharves. In 1997, an Australian stevedoring company set out to improve productivity by secretly training, in Dubai, a non union labour force of ex members of the Australian military. Dubai was chosen as the training location because it was highly efficient and did not have a labour union. The Maritime Union of Australia uncovered the subterfuge before the labour force got onto the site. It alerted the UAE ambassador to Australia of the plan and threatened to notify the International Labour Office (ILO) and have the port blacklisted. As a result, the members of the labour force en route to the site had their UAE visas cancelled at a stopover in Singapore. The embryonic work force was forced to abort the trip and return to Australia.

Other Emirates Before oil was discovered, the major port for the then Trucial States was located in the Emirate of Sharjah. After a storm deposited a sandbar at the mouth of the Sharjah creek, probably around the 1870s, the port of Sharjah became unserviceable and the existing port at Dubai became the focal point for trade in the region. Later, because of rivalry between the rulers of the individual emirates, Sharjah built Mina Khalid, a new container port, on reclaimed land.

Sharjah has another port in the east, on the Gulf of Oman, at Khor Fakkam. The port is located beyond the congested Straits of Hormuz and is one of the major trans-shipment facilities for the region. Khor Fakkam is one of three natural deep water harbours in the UAE.

The Port of Fujairah on the Gulf of Oman is one of the world's top three bunkering ports, the other two being Rotterdam and Singapore. Port charges are a major source of income for the emirate. Its two other deep water ports are at Diba and Kalba.

As a result of growth in the Umm al Qaiwain Free Zone, port facilities have been extended in this emirate.

The Emirate of Ras al Khaimah's main port is Mina Sagr, whose principal activity is trans-shipment to the region.

Extensive Roads, Highways and Freeways

The UAE has a superb network of roads, highways and freeways linking the emirates. Within the major centres, there are dual carriageways, tunnels and flyovers.

There are more than 3,000 kilometres (1864 miles) of good roads. However, once you travel away from the major centres, the roads are poor and a four-wheel drive vehicle is often required.

Some years ago, Abu Dhabi introduced traffic lights at most four way junctions. In Dubai, roundabouts are the principal device for traffic control but traffic lights are being progressively installed.

Camels on the Road

Visitors to the UAE may be amused to see, from time to time, camel warning road signs. If you see one, take it seriously. There have been collisions between cars and camels resulting in fatalities for both the occupants of the car and the camel. If you are travelling between Abu Dhabi and Dubai, you will observe that the highway is fenced. The fencing does not reflect ownership of the land; the fences have been built to keep camels off the highway.

Beware of Traffic Lights

In Dubai, some of the traffic lights at roundabouts only operate during peak periods. This can make crossing of the roads hazardous for pedestrians. Driving in the UAE is on the right-hand side of the road. This makes it more hazardous for visitors who are accustomed to vehicles driving on the left-hand side of the road.

Road signs are clearly marked in both Arabic and English.

Destinations and road name signs are in both Arabic and English. Addresses with street numbers and names are not well developed. When describing where you are or where you want to go, it is usually in reference to a prominent landmark.

There are no railways in the UAE.

Airports—Almost One Every Few Kilometres

Overview
The UAE is characterised by a certain measure of sibling rivalry. While the rulers are members of the same federal government, they are also the heads of state and the government for their particular emirates. Sibling rivalry manifests itself in the need to construct monuments that reflect the appropriate level of prestige in each emirate. Thus, the UAE is over serviced with six international airports—at Abu Dhabi, Dubai, Sharjah, Ras al Khaimah, Fujairah and Al Ain. More airlines fly in and out of the UAE than any other country in the world. In 2001, there were more than 90 airlines servicing the UAE. This compares to 66 airlines servicing Hong Kong.

Not only do most emirates have their own international airport, but Abu Dhabi, the wealthiest emirate has two—one at Abu Dhabi, the other at Al Ain opened in 1994. Pakistan International Airlines and six other airlines fly in and out of Al Ain International Airport. Almost all are airlines with a Middle Eastern base. Pakistan International Airlines carries a high number of Pakistanis working in Al Ain.

Abu Dhabi Abu Dhabi International Airport is located approximately 30 kilometres from the downtown area, some 160 kilometres away from Dubai and Sharjah International Airports. The number of international airports in fairly close proximity leads to duplication of services and inefficient competition for customers.

The new Rashid Terminal at Dubai International Airport is one of the world's most modern and user-friendly terminals, and arguably the world's best airport for duty-free shopping.

Thirty-five airlines fly in and out of Abu Dhabi International Airport. Of the 35 airlines, seven have bases in Europe, nine have bases in Asia and the other 19 airlines have bases in the region. Approximately three million passengers passed through Abu Dhabi International Airport in 2000 which has a city check-in facility with duty free shops.

Dubai The Emirate of Dubai has an open sky policy permitting any airline to fly into Dubai. Unlike Singapore's open sky policy requiring reciprocity, Dubai's policy is unconditional.

The principal airport for the UAE is Dubai, located five kilometres from the downtown area. In 2001, there were 95 airlines flying in and out of Dubai. Shaikh Rashid Terminal, one of its two terminals, receives the regular scheduled flights. Terminal Two receives chartered flights and some of the less well-known airlines, including those from the CIS. Approximately 25 airlines use Terminal Two. Dubai International Airport handled over 12 million passengers in 2000. The number of passengers passing through Dubai International Airport is about a third of Hong Kong's. In 2000, Dubai International Airport airfreighted nearly half a million tonnes of cargo. Again, this is about one third the volume of Hong Kong's airport.

Other Emirates Most passenger airlines flying into Sharjah Airport are from the CIS and the subcontinent. Landing charges in Sharjah are significantly lower than that in Abu Dhabi or Dubai. The disadvantages of Sharjah Airport are that there are relatively few international connections and flights do not arrive at the most convenient times. Complaining to the local newspaper, a resident of Sharjah bemoaned that flight arrival and departure times from Sharjah International Airport were always at bewitching hours.

Sharjah International Airport has an international free trade zone and is the biggest cargo-handling airport in the Middle East. International airlines such as Lufthansa and Singapore Airlines make Sharjah their cargo transit port because of the lower landing charges. Sharjah has plans to launch its own airline—Falcon Airlines. If this takes place, the UAE would have three international carriers: Emirate Airlines, linked with Dubai; Gulf Air, linked with Abu Dhabi; and Falcon Airlines, linked with Sharjah.

Nine airlines fly into Ras al Khaimah's International Airport located in the Al-Hamraniah district.

Three airlines fly into Fujairah International Airport. They include Gulf Air, Egypt Air and Indian Airlines.

Airlines

Dubai's award winning airline, Emirates Airlines was one of the first airlines to offer its passengers espresso and cappuccino coffee. Emirates Airlines flies to 53 destinations and operates a fleet of more than 30 Boeing 777s and Airbus A300s with an average age of 48 months.

Emirates Airlines belongs to the Emirates Group whose affiliates include DNATA which is the ground handling agent for all the airlines flying into Dubai. DNATA, established by the Dubai government, is one of the largest travel organisations in the Middle East. It also represents 26 offline airlines. The major shareholder in the Emirates Group is the Government of Dubai.

Recent developments have seen the formation of strategic alliances such as First World and Star Alliance by many of the world's major airlines. Emirates Airlines is a partner airline in the Skywards strategic alliance whose members include ANA, British Airways, Continental Airlines, South African Airways and United Airlines. Emirates Airlines has code share arrangements with, and manages, Sri Lankan Airlines.

> ### The Birth of Emirates Airlines
> Before the development of the Boeing 747-400, Bahrain, the UAE and Iran were refuelling stops for wide-bodied, long-range passenger aircraft travelling from Asia to Europe or Europe to Asia. The development of the Boeing 747-400 with its long-range fuel tanks meant that aircraft departing from Hong Kong, Singapore and Bangkok could be in the air for more than fourteen hours and fly over Bahrain, Dubai or Tehran non stop to London, Paris, Frankfurt and Amsterdam. This would have spelt disaster for the UAE and the Emirate of Dubai in particular. The ruler and the government turned this particular problem into an opportunity. They launched their own airline—Emirates Airlines. Today, it is Dubai's international airline flying to many long-range destinations with a modern fleet of aircraft.
>
> ### Do Race Horses Fly First Class?
> Singapore Airlines flies racehorses owned by the Dubai royal family as well as other racehorses to and from Dubai. What class do they fly?
> Not economy, business or first class which is for mere humans. They fly luxury class together with their minders, as they are millionaires in their own right. Singapore Airlines has other interesting *passengers*. Its mega-top Boeing 747-400 has the capacity to transport giraffes.

Gulf Air grew out of what was in the 1950s an affiliate of BOAC (now British Airways) to service the Gulf. The UAE's involvement is through the Emirate of Abu Dhabi's government having equity in the airline along with the governments of Bahrain, Qatar and Oman. Gulf Air is the national carrier of the four states. Unlike Emirates Airlines which is run on a strictly commercial basis, politics intrude into the management of Gulf Air. This manifests itself in a number of ways. The chairmanship of the airline rotates amongst the representatives of the four governments and it is believed that key management and flight deck appointments are not necessarily made strictly on merit as each country must have a proportion of these appointments. As Gulf Air is owned by a number of AGCC countries, in addition to Abu Dhabi, there could be a political dimension to flight routing.

Bahrain-based Gulf Air moved its global maintenance facility to Abu Dhabi with the formation of the Gulf Aircraft Maintenance Company (GAMCO), a joint venture between Gulf Air (40% equity) and the Abu Dhabi government (60% equity). GAMCO specialises in the servicing of Airbuses and Tri-stars. Its foreign customers include Britain's Royal Air Force.

Getting About

Limousines

Somewhat surprisingly for such an overtly wealthy country, one does not see many US-style stretched limousines. They are nonetheless available and can be hired at UAD 1,000 per day. On arrival in Abu Dhabi or Dubai, most hotels will transfer you to and from the airport by limousine or luxury mini bus. Five and four-star hotels also provide transportation to and from the major shopping centres (including the newly opened, larger than life City Centre in Dubai). Hotels also provide transportation to and from the nearby beaches. Many business travellers use the limousine service to travel between Abu Dhabi and Dubai.

Taxis

Taxis are the principal means of transport for visiting business people. There are plenty of taxis in the major business centres and they are relatively inexpensive. Some taxis do not have metres and you will need to negotiate the fare before commencing your journey. This can involve some haggling. In the authors' experience, fares quoted by drivers of taxis without meters are similar to, if not the same as, metered taxis. However, there was an occasion when the driver took us from Sharjah to Ajman and on finding that the destination was a five-star hotel, increased his fare from UAD10 to UAD 15. The concierge persuaded him that his action was inappropriate.

> **Honest UAE Taxi Drivers**
> A Lebanese national travelling in a taxi in Dubai left his wallet containing UAD 20,000 on the back seat. He called the Dubai Transport Corporation, giving the time, the place he boarded the taxi, and his destination. The Corporation was able to identify the taxi and he had his wallet returned to him. The taxi driver was commended for his honesty by the Dubai Transport Corporation and rewarded by the passenger.

In Abu Dhabi and Dubai, you will find that all the taxis are metered, extremely clean, the drivers uniformed, polite and very knowledgeable of the area. Most taxi drivers are subcontinent expatriates or non Gulf Arabs who have a good command of the English language. You are unlikely to encounter a taxi driver who is a UAE national.

> **How Much You Pay Depends on Your Nationality**
> An expatriate businessman hailed a taxi in Abu Dhabi and in the course of the conversation was asked by the driver if he was an American. On hearing, "No, I'm an Australian," the driver made a turn and drove in the opposite direction. The Australian may not have realised that Silver Top, a major Australian taxi company, has a strategic alliance with a fleet of taxis in the UAE.

Buses
There are many school buses and more than 500 public buses. Public buses are run mainly by municipal governments. Passengers are usually lower income workers from the subcontinent. Expatriate students are encouraged to use public buses with discounted passes. Relatively few UAE students use the public transport system.

In 2001, the municipal government of Dubai significantly expanded its fleet with 100 new buses. The buses were required to service new routes as a result of new industrial and residential developments as well as increase the frequency of services. Another reason for the increase in the bus fleet was the new 2001 labour laws which made it mandatory for workers in Dubai to be transported to and from work in buses rather than trucks.

Car Hire
Cars can be hired in all the major centres. In Dubai, daily rates are USD 39 for a Mazda 323, USD 60 for a Toyota Cressida, USD 86 for a Volvo 940, USD 121 for a Mercedes C 200 and USD 167 for a four-wheel Toyota Land Cruiser.

Abras
Abras are motorised water taxis that ply the Dubai Creek. They are used especially by subcontinent workers to travel from Bur Dubai to Deira, two regions in Dubai. The Dubai Creek separates the southern section of Bur Dubai, the city's traditional heart, from

A luxury launch and a traditional abra share the Dubai Creek.

the northern area of Deira. Most of the passengers are workers travelling to and from work.

Expatriate middle and senior management staff, and UAE nationals rarely use an abra to travel to and from work.

First World Quality Electricity Supply

Subsidies to manufacturing industry are provided by the government to encourage secondary industries to establish in the UAE.

Power is 220 volts and 50 Hz. Approximately half the electricity generated in the UAE is consumed by business and the other half by households.

The Emirate of Abu Dhabi subsidizes the cost of electricity up to 75% for UAE nationals, and up to 50% for businesses and households which are not UAE nationals. Like in many First World countries, the Abu Dhabi government is moving towards privatisation. From 1999 to 2010, the functions of the Water and Electricity Department will be progressively sold off to 11 private companies. Foreigners will be able to take equity in these companies. The rationale behind privatisation is the elimination of government subsidies. To meet future power demands in Abu Dhabi, a new power plant is to be built at Taweelah, in the Maqta district.

In the Emirate of Dubai, the Dubai Electricity and Water Authority provides for the needs of industry and consumers. It has been boosting power generation, particularly in the Jebel Ali Free Zone. Their major power station is at al Awir.

Sharjah uses natural gas supplied by BP-Amoco to generate electricity. To boost output, the Sharjah Electricity and Water Authority (SEWA) have purchased two gas turbines from the French company Alsthors for their WASIT Power Station and a new power plant is being installed at Layyah.

In Fujairah, wind and solar power is being used to generate electricity to light remote villages and it is planned that solar power will also be used to supply electricity to businesses and factories.

A federal ministry of electricity and water has been established to develop a UAE grid to meet the power needs of the poorer northern emirates.

Sourcing Cost-Effective Water

The Arabian Peninsula has no rivers. Since there is negligible rainfall in the UAE or surrounding areas, no surface water is available as a source for water supply but adequate water is available. Most of the water supply (80%) in the UAE is from desalination. This is very expensive and energy-intensive. There are underground water supplies but they are drying up. Approximately 70% of water resources are consumed by agriculture through irrigation. Government initiatives to obtain greater efficiency from water resources include improved irrigation techniques, ground water projects and the construction of dams.

A major supplier of desalinated water is the Dubai Aluminium Company (Dubal) which supplies approximately 70% of Dubai's fresh water. Seawater is heated and the vapour is trapped into colder condenser tubes. Every eight litres of seawater pumped into the desalination plant yields one litre of fresh water. Piped water is available throughout the major centres. Water has to be paid for, but subsidies are available to encourage businesses to locate in the UAE.

In the 1980s, the Emirate of Abu Dhabi commenced recycling water via the Mafraq Sewerage Treatment Plant. Over the period 1991 to 2001, an experiment by the Abu Dhabi Municipality in co-operation with the Japanese Government, explored the vapourization of underground saline water using solar energy in the Rahba farming district.

Water forms a feature in many buildings as it is a scarce resource.

Ground water initiatives include sinking over 50 wells in the Al Khazna Remah district between Al Ain and Abu Dhabi city. More dams are being built in valleys to tap rainwater. The Wadi al Basirah Dam in the Hajar Mountains was completed in 1999.

21st Century Telecommunications

Emirates Telecommunications Corporation (Etisalat) controls and manages telecommunications in the UAE. It is one of the largest public-listed companies in the AGCC, with the UAE government owning 60 % of the shares. In addition to operating in the UAE, Etisalat has undertaken projects in Zanzibar and the Sudan. Etisalat owns 34% of the UAE-based Al Thuraya Satellite Telecommunications Company and has 1% equity in Qatar Telecom. Etislat is a global player in telecommunications through its equity in ICO Global Communications. It has concluded a number of roaming deals with ICO Global Communications, the Saudi Telecommunication Company, Bahrain Telecommunication Company and the Kuwait Mobile Telecommunication Company. The roaming deals allow the cellular customers of all these companies to share the global satellite systems.

Etisalat has provided the UAE with an internet service since 1995, and gives free internet training to UAE nationals residing in Abu Dhabi or Dubai. In 1999, it launched Comtrust, an e-commerce service for online payment solutions. It is also in the business of manufacturing SMART and SIM cards. Digital technology has been introduced to all exchanges and an advanced fibre-optic network has enhanced performance and efficiency. Mobile phone ownership in 1998 was 17%.

In 1999, Etisalat established its cable TV network, E-Vision giving consumers a choice of over 100 channels.

Telecommunications and Marine Services FZE (E-Marine) is an affiliate of Etisalat and operates two cable ships to service the underwater cables.

The highrise Etisalat building in Dubai. Etisalat is the UAE's communications company providing satellite, internet, mobile and telephone services.

The General Postal Authority is responsible for mail service in the UAE. All mail is delivered to a post office box and not to a street address because residential properties are very rarely numbered. However, in Dubai, the Dubai Civil Defence Department has been co-ordinating with the Dubai Municipality to set up a plan for the numbering and naming of streets. This will facilitate the future delivery of mail to residences or offices. Apart from this, the postal system is modern and efficient. There has also been an upgrade in the automatic vending of stamps.

In addition to the General Postal Authority, there are a number of major international couriers and logistics management companies including DHL, Federal Express and TNT. The domestic company, Memo Express, is listed on the UAE stock exchange. In 2001, all the major logistics and courier companies announced expansion plans—reflecting high growth of package redistribution services in the UAE. The General Postal Authority has an affiliated company trading under the brand name Empost. Products offered by Empost include a door to door courier service, a direct mail marketing service and the sale of stationery items through franchised petrol stations. The basic strategy of these companies has been to offer customers a *trade made easy* import and export services.

If you are an American Express (Amex) cardholder or have American Express travellers cheques, the UAE Amex offices in Abu Dhabi and Dubai will hold mail on your behalf.

Education

Education offers marketing opportunities for businesses and employment opportunities for expatriates. Education is and will remain one of the highest expense areas of the federal budget.

At all levels of education—primary, secondary and tertiary—there is involvement of both government and private sectors.

Private schools and universities enjoy a fair degree of autonomy. They can appoint their staff, develop their curriculum and make their term holidays. The government exercises indirect control through the need for all private schools to be licensed, and indirect control over overseas staff appointments through the issue or non issue of visas and work permits.

Tertiary institutions include universities, higher colleges of technology and specialist colleges.

Government Control of Private Schools

The government wanted to have all private schools change their weekend from Friday and Saturday, to Thursday and Friday. It effected the weekend change by threatening to revoke the licences of schools which were not willing to comply with the government's request.

Most teachers at primary and secondary schools, and lecturers at tertiary institutions are expatriates. The government is moving towards significantly increasing the number of UAE nationals in the teaching service.

Recruitment of Lecturers for Higher Colleges of Technology

Positions are advertised in overseas newspapers. On receipt of the candidate's CV, a video interview is conducted amongst shortlisted candidates. The video is then shown to a selection committee in the UAE. Successful candidates are then offered a specific position at a specific campus. Candidates do not have to take up the first offer. Offers are usually made twice a year and the candidate can wait until a campus of his or her choice is offered. On taking up the offer, there is scope for salary negotiations within specific bands. As with all employees in the UAE, salaries are tax free. The college then arranges a resident visa and a work permit for the successful candidate, and provides housing or a housing allowance as required by the law for all expatriates. Probation period is one year.

There are two domestic universities and a number of overseas universities and colleges with campuses in the UAE. The Australian-based University of Wollongong markets itself as the only branch of an overseas university awarding business degrees in the Gulf. The American University of Sharjah claims that it has the highest standards in the Gulf. There are two local universities: the University of the United Arab Emirates was opened in 1997,

Undergraduates use the library at the Dubai Women's College.

and Zayed University in 2000. The University of the United Arab Emirates at Al Ain announced a UAD 65 million project to build a university town. The concept is to bring together all the elements of the university that are spread out in different areas of Al Ain. There are no student digs at the University of the United Arab Emirates. Accommodation is of five-star hotel standards and includes a health club and a large shopping centre. There are approximately 10,000 undergraduate and postgraduate students attending universities in the UAE.

Complementing the universities are the higher colleges of technology with campuses in each emirate. Other tertiary institutions include the police academies and colleges specialising in travel, tourism, and medicine.

Businesses also have a direct involvement in tertiary education. DNATA (part of the Emirates Group) is involved in travel and tourism and hires a significant number of UAE nationals who have graduated from Skyline College in Sharjah. Skyline College is affiliated with the National American University. It offers specialist courses in travel and tourism, marketing, international business and hospitality management. DNATA's affiliate, Emirates Airlines, has its own Aviation College and a joint venture with the University of Bradford which offers a customised executive MBA. Aviation College is also unique because of its architecture. The college building is in the shape of the fuselage of a Boeing 777.

Zayed University and the headquarters of the higher colleges of technology are located in Abu Dhabi.

The universities and the higher colleges of technology have been collaborating with the business sector to develop educational programmes that meet the needs of business. The idea is to ensure that graduates will be able to make an immediate contribution to their employer's bottom line. One such programme is the Industrial Training Programme. Engineering students are regularly sent overseas to work for brief periods with major companies like Dassault Aviation, GIAT Industries and Thompson CSF. Many of the higher colleges also offer short-term courses to UAE nationals and residents on business-related subjects. The fees for a short-term course are approximately UAD 25 per hour.

Approximately two-thirds of kindergartens, primary and secondary schools are government-run, although private schools make up 40% of the student population. Nearly one quarter of a million students attend primary schools where attendance is compulsory and free. Secondary education is not compulsory and government statistics show that there are approximately 145,000 students enrolled in both academic and vocational streams. The UAE had some 640 government schools in 1999.

For dependent children of expatriates, there are a number of international schools. These follow the British, French, Indian or American curriculum. Most expatriate executives have, as part of their remuneration package, provision for private school fees to be paid by their employer.

Australia plays an important role in education in the UAE. The Australian State of Victoria has provided a complete educational package to primary and secondary schools in the UAE.

An outcome of higher educational standards is the government's need to find jobs for the increasing number of UAE nationals who complete high school each year, and graduate from universities and other higher colleges of technology.

Spending on education represents between 2% and 5% of GDP and is likely to rise because of the increasing percentage of school-going UAE nationals. The government also gives financial assistance to UAE nationals studying overseas.

Adult literacy is 85%. There are a number of illiteracy eradication centres throughout the UAE, and the government is willing to open an illiteracy centre even for one person. The highest level of illiteracy is amongst women.

Sharjah is regarded as the cultural capital of the UAE because its ruler is an academic.

Living in the UAE

Accommodation

Short-term business visitors usually stay in four or five-star hotels. Hilton, Hyatt, Inter-Continental, Meridian, Rydges, Sheraton and other international hotels all have properties in the major centres with world class business and conference facilities. In Dubai, there is the opportunity to stay at beach hotels that offer top class leisure and recreational facilities, including water sports; and serviced apartments. One-bedroom apartments at the Hyatt Regency are UAD 7,000 to 8,000 a month, and two-bedroom apartments at UAD 80,000 per annum.

Western businessmen who visit the UAE regularly and stay for longer periods often rent a studio apartment to avoid the high tariffs at hotels. In Dubai, studio apartments are available on a monthly lease of approximately UAD 5,000 per month.

Where accommodation is not provided by the employer, expatriate middle managers or supervisors living in the UAE will find that the cost of renting a house or apartment can be up to 50% of their salary.

A wide range of accommodation options ranging from large, serviced and non-serviced apartments, to villas is available. The newer villas have enclosed compounds with a security guard and a swimming pool. Most leased apartments provide a 24-hour security service. An unusual feature of swimming pools in the UAE is that they are covered and the water has to be cooled because of the extremely high temperatures in summer.

If you are taking up an appointment with your family in the UAE, you will find Dubai a popular choice of most western expatriates. The most up-market residential area in Dubai is Jumeirah Beach, where the cost of leasing a villa ranges from UAD 100,000 to UAD 300,000 per year.

An expatriate manager's residence in the upmarket Dubai suburb of Jumeirah.

A less expensive area offering 3 to 4-bedroom villas is the Mirdiff area, where rents range from UAD 60,000 to UAD 90,000. For those preferring non serviced apartments, Shaikh Zayed Road and the area behind the Burgeman Shopping Centre offer a wide choice.

Some western expatriates who work in Dubai choose to live in Sharjah, a twenty to thirty minutes' drive away from Dubai. The cost of housing in Sharjah is lower than in Dubai. A villa can be leased from between UAD 50,000 to UAD 200,000 per year. Sharjah is also the location of many of the manufacturing businesses in the UAE.

Expatriate supervisors and managers from the subcontinent have commented on how difficult it is to house hunt in the UAE. Their particular complaint is that advertisements for houses and apartments are misleading. Landlords tell customers that apartments have all amenities with large rooms but on inspection, the rooms are small and do not have all the amenities that were advertised. To add insult to injury, the landlord often requests a refundable deposit from the subcontinent manager or supervisor before being shown the apartment.

The Arenco Option
There is a company in Dubai called Arenco which will lease you almost anything for your apartment or villa. This is especially useful if one's company refuses to pay for shipping costs for household furniture. Items available for rent include anything from a video cassette recorder to household furniture. Office furniture, desks, filing cabinets and other equipment can also be leased.

Public housing used to be available from the Dubai municipality managing some residential blocks. This has now been privatised. Tenants have complained about the increase in rents and the falling standards of maintenance since privatisation.

Rents are normally paid in advance for the duration of the lease. This means that if you lease an apartment or villa for 12 months as most expatriate families do, an advance of 12 months' rent must be paid at the beginning of the lease period. In addition, a security deposit will normally be required. There have been recent trends for landlords to accept rent on a half-yearly or quarterly basis, but only if they receive post-dated cheques for the amount for the balance of the lease period. A word of warning: it is a criminal offence to write cheques that are dishonoured.

If you decide to lease a fully serviced apartment, you will find that these apartments are also popular with short-term visitors from other AGCC countries, including Saudi Arabia. Vacationing families from Saudi Arabia tend to be very boisterous in places like Dubai where there is access to alcohol and other delights of the west.

When leasing an apartment or villa, make sure that there is a clear understanding with the real estate agent or the landlord as to who is responsible for maintenance.

Most western expatriates use bottled water for drinking, cooking, making tea and coffee, and even cleaning their teeth.

Domestic Help

Most expatriates employ domestic help; maids from Sri Lanka speak exceptionally good English. Live-in maids are paid approximately UAD 1,000 per month and airfare for travel to and from their home country once a year. For those not wanting a live-in maid, there are companies which provide part-time cleaners. Drivers are also available.

Driving

Although the UAE recognizes some foreign driving licences, including those issued in the UK, it is best to obtain an international driving licence before you arrive in the UAE. Many UAE companies have a *Mr Fixit* who will facilitate the issue of your

UAE driving licence. Expatriate executives normally have a company car, which is bought rather than leased, as part of their remuneration package.

> ### If You Don't Have a Recognized Driving Licence
> You have to go back to basics, take driving lessons and sit a driving test. When you pass, you will have to take another test to see if you understand road signals in the UAE, and an eye test. Women are tested by policewomen and males by policemen. As there are more male applicants than female applicants for a driving licence, it usually takes men longer to secure appointments for the various tests while women can generally obtain a driver's licence within a shorter period.
>
> Driving tests are not taken in your own car. The government supplies a car and four candidates are tested at the same time. Most of the country is flat, but the testing stations have an artificial hill to test your parking skills.
>
> ### How the UAE Perceives the Number of Motor Vehicle Accidents and Traffic Density
> Blue-collar expatriates from the subcontinent are often discriminated against by UAE nationals and western expatriates. They find it especially hard to obtain driving licences, as the traffic police repeatedly fails them. The rationale for this is that if too many licences are issued to blue-collar expatriates from the subcontinent, these expatriates will obtain jobs as truck drivers and chauffeurs, thus increasing the number of drivers on the road and the number of accidents.

Cars in Dubai drive on the right-hand side of the road. The road system in the UAE is good, but driving can be an intimidating experience for non residents and even residents. A common practice for UAE nationals is to depress the accelerator pedal and put their life in the hands of God, letting the car go where it wants to go. This technique is called the *inshallah* method of driving.

People drive more aggressively, show less regard to speed restrictions and sound their horn more frequently.

It is all too easy to meet with an accident in the UAE. One of the most dangerous roads is the Ras al Khaimah-Umm al Quaiwain road. Statistics show that one person is killed on this road each week. In an accident, the police decide on the spot the cause of the blame and the party responsible for the damage. If you are an expatriate involved in an accident, you will most likely be found the guilty party on the grounds that the accident would not have occurred had you been somewhere else. The same principle of justice is not normally applied to UAE nationals. If you are involved in an accident, you should not move your car (even if it obstructs the traffic) until the police have attended to the case. There is one exception: if the damage is minor, no one is injured and both parties are in agreement, the car can be moved. Bear in mind that no motor workshop or mechanic will repair a motor vehicle without a police certificate.

The speed limit on the Abu Dhabi to Dubai freeway is 120 kilometres per hour but most cars travel at 150 kilometres per hour.

One of the factors contributing to a higher than average accident rate in the UAE is the way the traffic lights operate. In Abu Dhabi, there is no pause between the red light in one direction and the green light in the other direction. As a result, drivers have difficulty stopping in time at intersections. In Dubai, an amber light shows before the traffic lights turn from green to red. The purpose of the amber light is to warn the driver to slow down before the light turns red. UAE nationals completely misinterpret the amber light. They see the amber light as an opportunity to speed through the intersection and beat the lights. Another contributing factor is the lack of a police presence. The authors did not see a police vehicle at the many roundabouts on their recent visit.

The Expatriate Manager who Got into Trouble with the Car Rental Company

A newly arrived expatriate manager drove his rented car to the supermarket. While parked at the supermarket, it was hit by another car. The manager did not notice the damage. When he returned the car, the rental company drew his attention to the minor damage and asked for his police certificate. The car rental company was mortified to learn that there was no police certificate as it meant that the car could not be repaired and leased out again.

A Lucky Break

Drinking and driving is a big *no no* in the UAE. Many western countries have drink driving laws that prohibit people with blood alcohol levels of 0.05% from driving. In the UAE, there is no legal level but it is an offence to be drunk whilst driving. The usual definition of drunken driving is to have the smell of alcohol on the driver's breath. An expatriate manager, driving home after a few beers at his club, was pulled over by the police for a routine inspection of registration and licences. He panicked but the police were only interested in the particular job assigned to them—to check his registration and licence.

Go Faster

Speed limits are not observed in the UAE. The wife of an expatriate general manager underwent a driving test. Her instructor criticised her for driving too slowly. She protested that her speedometer showed 60 kilometres per hour and to go faster would be breaking the speed limit. Her instructor said, *"It does not matter. You are driving too slowly."*

Personal Finances

Many personal purchases are paid for in cash. This is because the penalties for writing a dishonoured cheque in the UAE are high. A dishonoured cheque gets you a warning; a second dishonoured cheque, and it's off to jail you go. The law also requires that your cheque account have a minimal balance of UAD 2500.

It is fairly easy to obtain a loan to acquire assets such as a car but it is relatively more difficult for an expatriate to obtain a personal loan.

Sports and Recreation

Dubai is the sporting capital of the Middle East, attracting world class sportsmen to international sporting events. These events include the world's richest horse race—the Dubai World Cup. In fact, the Dubai World Cup has been compared to the Arc de Triomphe, Royal Ascot and the Melbourne Cup. The Dubai World Cup is held at the Nad Al Sheeba race course, about a twenty-minute drive from downtown Dubai.

Dubai has three world class golf courses. The Dubai Desert Classic Golf Tournament and the ATP-approved Dubai Tennis Open attracts many sporting celebrities, including Tiger Woods. In 2001, the prize money for the Dubai Desert Classic was £1,000,000. The Dubai Aluminium Company (Dubal) was the major sponsor for the Dubai Desert Classic— its rationale being that Dubai is a key international player in the aluminium industry and the Dubai Desert Classic complements that role. The event promoter is the Dubai World Trade Centre.

Other significant sporting events include the Dubai Rugby Seven Tournament, the UIM Class One world offshore power boat championship, the Dubai International Rally, the UAE Desert Challenge for car drivers, the FEI International Show Jumping Competition and the World Equestrian Games Endurance Race for Horse Riders. Sharjah is the home of the International Cricket Competition.

There are numerous sporting clubs in the UAE and club membership for a family is normally part of the expatriate manager's remuneration package. In addition to these clubs, the five-star hotels allow the use of their facilities such as the swimming pool and gymnasium to expatriate families for a *club* fee.

Safety

The UAE is one of the safest countries in the Middle East. However, the crime rate is higher than reported as, according to many western expatriates, some crimes involving UAE nationals go unreported.

Restaurants do not bring in their outside furniture when they close as no one will steal it.

CHAPTER 5

Evaluating Opportunities

Visiting the Market

If you want to visit the UAE you will most probably need a sponsor and a visa. For regular business visitors their master distributor, commercial agent or joint venture partner normally arranges the sponsorship and the visa.

Not everyone requires a sponsor to arrange a visa. British passport holders and citizens of AGCC countries can enter the UAE and be issued immediately with a visa valid for one month. The AGCC countries include Bahrain, Kuwait, Oman, Qatar and Saudi Arabia. The British have favoured status because of a reciprocal agreement; UAE nationals can enter the UK without a visa.

If you are visiting the UAE for the first time, there are a number of ways you can obtain sponsorship and a visa. Your travel agent can make the arrangements through your hotel, which will charge the travel agent a fee for arranging your sponsorship and visa. This will be passed on to you. Hotels impose a charge for this service because they incur real costs. The hotel will need to make at least two trips to the immigration department to obtain your visa, and this will cost them at least UAD 70. The visa itself costs UAD 100. In addition, a UAD 10 "lodgement fee" is levied. Hotels also add a fee, ranging from UAD 180, for making the arrangements. You must allow six working days for processing the sponsorship and visa paperwork. If you need a sponsor and a visa urgently, an additional fee of UAD 280 ensures that the visa is issued in 36 hours.

You will not have to go through a travel agent to obtain a sponsorship and a visa. If you know where you want to stay, you can approach the hotel directly to sponsor you and arrange for your visa. The hotel will ask you for a clear copy of the passport information page which has your photo to ensure that it has the correct passport details. To confirm this information, it will send you its hotel visa application form which has a few additional questions such as your parents' names, your religion and your qualifications.

Another way to obtain sponsorship and a visa is to fly into Dubai on Emirates Airlines. Emirates has a business unit specialising in visa services, staffed by UAE nationals who are authorised to act on behalf of the Department of Immigration and Naturalisation. There is no charge for a visa if you are staying in Dubai for less than 96 hours.

Before you depart for the UAE, make sure you have a copy of your visa. You will probably require this to board your flight. On arrival at your UAE port of entry, proceed to the immigration area where there are visa collection desks. When you produce your copy of the visa, the original will be issued to you. You can then proceed to immigration and customs.

> **Marhaba or First Class Service**
> DNATA, the sole ground handling agent at Dubai International Airport, offers travellers a premium meet-and-greet service. For a fee, you will be met by a hostess, be transported around the airport terminal in a special buggy, receive priority immigration treatment and have the use of its opulent lounges. The fee for use of the lounges is USD16.

When visiting the UAE on business, make sure your passport is "clean". An Israeli visa in your passport will prevent you from entering the UAE. Likewise, it can be so for a UAE visa in Israel. When Margaret, one of the authors, visited Israel after visiting the Gulf states, including the UAE, she was grilled by Israeli emigration officials before leaving Israel. They wanted to know why she was in the Gulf states and the UAE. Her travel companion was also extensively questioned to corroborate her story and to confirm that she was not an agent for the enemies of Israel.

> **Passport Tip**
> If your children's details are included in your passport, make sure you have your children with you when you approach the immigration counter.

Most business people enter the UAE on a visit visa valid for one month. This can be extended a further month. Another one month period of grace is allowed so that it is possible to stay for up to three months on a visit visa. After three months, you will be fined for each day you stay in the UAE illegally.

It used to be the case that if you wanted to change your visa status, you had to leave the country and then come back on your new UAE visa status. This is no longer the requirement. If you qualify for a changed visa status, you can remain in the UAE for an administrative fee of UAD 500 to the Ministry of Interior.

Supplying the Globe

Many companies perceive the UAE as a small market but it should be noted that Dubai is a business hub with substantial re-exports. Although the economy has diversified away from oil, growth of manufacturing industry is somewhat limited by the size of the domestic market. Products manufactured in the UAE include textiles, consumer goods and construction products.

In exploring the UAE market, you should examine carefully how marketing in the UAE fits with your company's global, regional and Gulf business strategy.

The first step is to make contact with your home country's trade commissioner or the consular's commercial section. Some countries, such as Australia, maintain state government business offices in the UAE. Of the six states of Australia, three of the most populous and economically wealthier states, namely Queensland, New South Wales and Victoria, have established government business offices in the UAE.

Other useful initial contacts are your bank if it has offices in the UAE and your shipping company if its vessels sail to the UAE.

In the UAE, there are also a number of foreign chambers of commerce such as British Business in the Gulf, in addition to the emirate chambers of commerce. Your home city may have an Arab Chamber of Commerce or its equivalent which may be able to provide you with some business information on the UAE.

Emerging and Developing Industries

Quarrying and Downstream Businesses

The cement industry was one of the first industries to be established in the UAE when the Al Ittihod Cement Company opened for business in Ras al Khaimah in 1975. One of the world's largest rock quarrying operations is undertaken near the town of Khor Khuwaii in the Emirate of Ras al Khaimah. The limestone quarried from the Hajar Mountains is of high quality and is transported via barges to other locations in the UAE or is crushed on site to make cement at the plants close to the quarry. The Ras al Khaimah Cement Company has five plants in the emirate and is the only location where white cement is manufactured.

Fujairah, being the emirate with the rockiest soil conditions, also has a significant quarrying industry and a downstream ceramics factory and rock wool factory. Rock wool is a material that can be used as a substitute for soil to grow plants, and is a material used by the construction industry. The ceramics factory makes glazed tiles. The rock wool factory produces mattresses for green house cultivation and supplies the construction industry with fill material. Fujairah also has a factory producing portland cement. In the Dibba region, there is a marble manufacturing plant.

The rock formations at Jebel Hatif, Jebel Mleiha and Wadi Haqil in Sharjah are of commercial value. They have been converted into cement, marble and rock wool. Sharjah also has a cement plant where limestone, quarried from Jebel Mleiha, is burnt in a kiln fired with Sharjah gas to produce clinker which is then ground down to make cement.

Other cement facilities are at Al Ain in the Emirate of Abu Dhabi. Factories in the Emirates of Ajman and Umm al Qaiwain produce portland cement.

Dubai's cement plant is at Jebel Ali. There are now eleven cement factories in the UAE and all raw materials, with the exception of gypsum and some additives, are available in the UAE.

An export business based on aggregates (the broken stones and other materials to make concrete) has been established.

Replacing Food Imports

The government's agricultural policy is to lessen the country's dependence on food imports. The agricultural and fishing sectors of the UAE economy accounted for 2.5% of GDP in 2001. Approximately 5% of the land in the UAE is cultivated, much of which is irrigated. Food produced in the UAE accounted for approximately 25% of total food consumption in 2001. Land reclamation and use of desalinized water make the UAE self sufficient in most of its fruit and vegetable needs. Since 1977, there has been a steady increase in the number of farms. Production of field crops, vegetables and fruits has increased. In areas with higher rainfall, date palms and mangoes are grown together with wheat and millet. Many are surprised to learn that tobacco is grown in the UAE.

Many farms have received government assistance in their establishment. Often, government agricultural officers develop a farm and then hand it over to a UAE national when it becomes viable. Even after the farm is in private hands, the government continues with its assistance, providing agricultural consultants, free veterinary services and subsidies for the purchase of fertilizer, seeds and pesticides.

There are well developed poultry and dairy farms at Falaj al Moalla in the Emirate of Umm al Qaiwain.

> **Can Shepherds be Persuaded to Change the Way They Feed their Sheep?**
> Shepherds are very conservative and feed their sheep only grain. Grain upsets the PH balance in the sheep's stomach causing them to scour or purge. The problem can easily be solved by feeding the sheep a diet supplement, but UAE shepherds don't because they believe that to use a feed supplement is not the will of Allah.

Agriculture One of the problems the country faces is the lack of rainwater for crops. This is exacerbated by the exhaustion of ground water.

The economy of Ras al Khaimah is based on agriculture. In 1955, the Government of Ras al Khaimah established an agricultural trial station to find out which crops would grow best in the harsh UAE climate. A School of Agriculture was established. This led to the development of commercial farms in the Digdagga area of Ras al Khaimah. These farms now grow lettuce, beans and maize for the European market. Agricultural centres in Ras al Khaimah with orchards are at Al-Hamraniah and Masafi. In Ras al Khaimah and Fujairah, dates are still a major crop. Other fruits grown in these emirates include oranges, lemons, limes, figs, mangoes, bananas, grapes and pomegranates. Alfalfa, a crop to feed animals, is also grown. Tomatoes and cucumbers are grown hydroponically—a method where plants are grown in plastic tubes without soil.

A French company, Giat Industries, has recently established a joint venture with Al Wathba Marionnet to clone date palms. It is anticipated that 50% of the cloned date palms will be exported.

The desert gives way to lush foliage.

In the Emirate of Abu Dhabi, agriculture centres on the town of Al Ain. There is an underground system of tunnels, known as falaj, to ensure a steady stream of water to irrigate the crops. An experimental farm of 1,000 hectares has been established to grow wheat, vegetables and horticultural products. As a result of the experiments there, Abu Dhabi now has more than 1,000 commercial farms. Dairy farms produce 37,000 tonnes of milk per year for consumption within the UAE.

The ruler's representative in the western region of the Emirate of Abu Dhabi has put in place a programme, scheduled for completion in 2010, that will have more than 3,000 farms developed in the Liwa, Ghiyathi, Bida Zayed and Al Ajban districts. The project's completion should see about 15,000 farms, covering an area of more than 100,000 hectares, in the western region.

In 1997, the National Horticulture Management Company was formed to provide marketing and technical assistance to farmers. In 1999, as part of a strategy to develop high value-added agri-business products, Franserre-UAE, in collaboration with Dassault Investment, Thomson Compensation International and Al Hamed Enterprises, began to market cut flowers. In addition to supplying the UAE market, the cut flowers are exported to Asia, Europe and the Middle East under the *Shams* brand name. The flowers are grown at Sweihan, in the Emirate of Abu Dhabi.

The Arid Land Research Centre was established on Saadiyat Island, in the Emirate of Abu Dhabi, in 1972, with a brief to experiment with hydroponic agriculture.

Crops are also cultivated in the Emirate of Fujairah where rainfall is high and there is an abundance of underground water. At the northern end of Fujairah, the historic town of Dibba is an important agricultural centre. The town of Siji has flower farms and the blooms are exported to Europe.

Sharjah also has an agricultural centre at the Dhoud Oasis where vegetables and fruits are grown on about a hundred farms, using greenhouse cultivation.

In the Emirate of Ajman, Masfut, some 110 kilometres southeast of Ajman City, is a centre for agriculture.

Flowers are grown and exported to Europe from the UAE.

The gardens at a hotel frequented by north European tourists.

Fishing The UAE has the third largest fishing fleet in the Gulf after Iraq and Oman, and the fourth largest fish catch in the Arab world. More than 114,000 tonnes of fish were caught in 1997.

The long-term prospects for the fishing fleet are somewhat uncertain because of pollution that has threatened fish stocks, causing a declining catch per fishing boat. The fishing industry is highly regulated. Under Federal Law 23 of 1999, commercial fishing boats need to be licensed and to display their number plates. The government also regulates the sale of commercial fishing boats and the number of people who are allowed to fish. Fishing boat crew must have a sailor's card or a worker's card, and only full time fishermen can have their permits renewed. Other regulations require that a UAE national be on board a commercial fishing boat when it is out fishing. (There were reports in 2001 that Ras al Khaimah had UAE nationals allowing subcontinent expatriates to go fishing commercially without their UAE sponsor on board.)

UAE nationals can own no more than two commercial fishing boats, and employ no more than two workers on each boat. To further protect the fishing industry, the Ministry of Agriculture and Fisheries introduced regulations that prohibit fishing during the spawning season and banning fishing for shrimps using the *hayala* fishing technique, where a 1500 metre net is used.

The Emirate of Umm al Qaiwain supplies most of the fish to the UAE. In the 1980s, the government, with Japanese assistance, established a marine resources and research centre to investigate prawn and other commercial fish farming.

The Emirate of Sharjah has territories in the east facing the Gulf of Oman and there are fishing villages near the towns of Kalba and Khor Kalba. Its government, together with Arizona University, has developed a large experimental salt water farm. This has led to the development of salt water farms in Abu Dhabi.

Fujairah, on the Gulf of Oman, has also a significant fishing industry. To increase fish stocks, the Dibba and Al Fujairah Municipality has developed some artificial caves on the marine reefs, 800 metres offshore.

In 1999, the International Fish Farming Company (Asmak) was incorporated. The major players behind it are the UAE Offset Group, Oasis National Food Company (an affiliate of the Abu Dhabi Investment Company), Union Cold Stores, Dassault Investments, Baldwin International Limited and Gulf Investments Corporation. Greek-based Nireus Chios Aquaculture SA has equity in the company and the management contract. Asmak is building two hatcheries in Abu Dhabi, and a fish fin and shrimp hatchery in the northern emirates. It signed a fish farming agreement with the government of Ras al Khaimah to lease 450 hectares, eight kilometres offshore from the Al Mataf district, for cage farming. Fish harvested will be exported to Europe and Japan.

Although there has been a general policy to replace imported food products, at the same time there is a demand for imported premium western gourmet foods, especially in Dubai.

Travel and Tourism

The tourist season in the UAE is from October to March. On an average, European tourists stay three weeks for the three S's—sun, sea and sand. Tourists from Asia are attracted to the UAE and Dubai, in particular, for a fourth S—shopping. No tourists enter the UAE for the S of some Asian destinations—sex.

The Emirate of Dubai is unquestionably the tourist capital of the Middle East. Dubai boasts that it has the world's lowest priced duty free shops. Items of value to purchase in the UAE include watches, luggage and ladies' handbags.

Dubai has been marketing itself as a short term rest and recreational centre for business executives travelling from Europe to East Asia, and they usually stay in the Jumeirah beach area where most of the vacation hotels are located. Expatriate residents in Abu Dhabi, Dubai and Sharjah often like to visit the resort town of Hatta for a short term vacation because Hatta can be used as a base to explore the nearby wadis, or desert canyons, and mountains.

A tourist beach hotel in Ajman.

In difficult economic times, other AGCC nationals, particularly those from Saudi Arabia and Kuwait, find a Europe vacation less attractive, financially. As an alternative, they visit the UAE and stay in Dubai.

Tourism in Dubai is projected to overtake oil as a major source of income in the next few years. In 1998, Dubai had 255 hotels with over 17,000 rooms. The Emirate of Dubai's Department of Tourism and Commerce Marketing has offices in many overseas countries, including the US, UK, France, Germany, Italy, Japan and Hong Kong.

Dubai is going full steam ahead to be the cruise capital of the Gulf. In 2001, there were 40 calls by cruise ships compared to only eight in 1996.

Many tourist hotels in the UAE have been built along the beaches north of Al Khan, in Sharjah. Of particular interest to tourists and business travellers to Sharjah is the central souq—a kind of Arab regional shopping centre that houses some 600 shops. Throughout the UAE, there are souqs that range from traditional to the very modern. Sharjah has been slow to develop as a destination for European tourists because of the ban on the consumption of alcohol in hotels. Sharjah has historically had this ban because it is a condition of Saudi Arabia's contribution to its economy. The ban will soon be removed and this should stimulate the growth of tourists from Europe.

The Emirate of Ras al Khaimah is attracting more tourists, especially Scandinavians on packaged tours. A popular tourist destination is the town of Khatt in Ras al Khaimah because of its thermal springs.

Fujairah, on the Gulf of Oman, has the most striking landscape. There are mountains, excellent diving sites and cultural attractions. The government has identified Aqq for the development of resort hotels and has entered into a joint venture with the Dubai-based Emirates Group to develop one. The Al

Mulla Group, Al Futtaim Group, the Rotana Group, and Abu Dhabi National Hotels have also expressed an interest in developing resort hotels in Fujairah.

Ras al Khaimah and Fujairah are like Hatta. They are popular weekend destinations for more affluent expatriates residing in the UAE.

In the Emirate of Abu Dhabi, the Abu Dhabi National Hotel Corporation (ADNHC) plays a key role in generating the tourist dirham. ADNHC owns six hotels and manages seven others. Its other business activities include managing the Abu Dhabi ice rink, the duty free complexes at the Abu Dhabi and Al Ain international airports and the Al Ghazal transport service company.

The four and five-star hotels in the UAE are managed by international chains such as the Hilton, Hyatt, Inter-Continental, Meridien, Rydges and Sheraton, but owned by UAE nationals and the royal families. One notable exception is the five-star hotel chain known as the Jemeriah Group (whose properties include the extraordinary Burj al Arab) which is both owned and managed by interests associated with the Dubai royal family.

DNATA (part of the Emirates Group that own Emirates Airlines) is the largest travel management service company in the UAE. Its affiliate, Emirates Holidays, is the largest tour operator in the Middle East.

Emirates Airlines has developed an eco-tourist facility—Al Maha Resort, some 45 minutes' travel from Dubai International Airport. At the resort, you will find Arabian oryx, also known in Arabic as Al Maha, and other wild life such as gazelles and foxes.

The UAE sees tourism as the way ahead. In 2000, there were some three million visitors, of whom 100,000 were tourists. The UAE now focuses on attracting quality tourists, and dissuades backpackers and those going for cheap packages.

Ship Building, Boat Building and Ship Repairing

The Abu Dhabi Ship Building Company (ADSB) is primarily concerned with building, refitting and repairing vessels for the UAE navy. ADSB, with its shipyard at Mussafah, evolved in 1995 as a result of an Offset programme with the US-based Newport News Shipbuilding Company holding 40% of the stock, the Emirate Government of Abu Dhabi holding 20% of the stock and UAE nationals holding the remaining 40%. Its projects have included the building and refitting of UAE navy patrol boats and the construction of fire-fighting tug boats for the UAE coastguard and navy. Another of its activities is the development of software packages for the UAE navy's fleet management programmes.

Also at Mussafah is Adyard Abu Dhabi whose principal operation is servicing the oil industry's marine equipment. Adyard's parent company is Oman-based Topaz Energy and Marine Saog. Specific projects undertaken by the parent company have included the refurbishment of drilling rigs and the construction of service barges.

In Sharjah, Maritime Industrial Services undertook a project in 1999 to convert a conventional ship into a jack-up oil rig.

The Dubai dry docks are one of the world's largest, capable of handling the largest tankers in the world.

Boat building in the UAE centres around the Emirate of Ajman. It is famous for building dhows using traditional methods. At any one time, there are approximately 40 dhows at various stages of construction. The dhows are not only sold in the UAE but to other Gulf States as well. Traditional dhows are also built in the Bateen area of Abu Dhabi City. Commercial dhows built today are used as short haul cargo vessels.

In addition to traditional boat building, Ajman has become a centre for the construction of speedboats and leisure craft. Gulf Craft claims 60% to 70% of the UAE boat market and exports constitute nearly 75% of the boats built. The 30,000 dwt dry dock vessel, Al Zora, was commissioned in 2001. The dry dock is owned by Arab Heavy Industries whose shareholders include the Ajman Government, the Dubai-based Al Futtaim Group and Singapore's Keppel Corporation.

The government-owned Dubai Drydocks Company is one of the largest dry dock facilities in the world, with ship repair facilities. Tasks undertaken by the Dubai Drydocks Company include the cleaning, repainting and repair of ships and the maintenance of heavy offshore oil equipment such as jack-up platforms, derricks and pipe laying barges. The Dubai Drydocks Company has recently diversified into the expanding aluminium fast boat market, constructing a 27-metre vessel for Mutawa Marine in Abu Dhabi.

Smaller vessels, including dhows, fishing boats and leisure craft are repaired at the Dubai ship docking yard at Al Jadaf.

Hollywood in the Desert

Ajman is the centre in the UAE for film processing and film-making. Studios produce movies and shows for TV in the UAE, the Gulf and the wider Arab community. Egyptian film makers have also used the film studios in Ajman.

Since the 1980s foreign film makers and, in particular, those from India (better known as *bollywood*) have featured Dubai and

Sharjah in their films and soap operas. The making of movies in the UAE has been given a boost by the recent popularity of Hindi satellite television where well known drama serials, *Daastan* and *Chattham*, feature Dubai and Sharjah on a regular basis. Bollywood film producers are drawn to the UAE by the availability of local production teams and the visual splendour of the emirates.

Mega movie stars such as Jean Claude van Damme have promised to make a movie in Dubai but this has yet to happen. A recent rumour had Hollywood planning to make a movie in the UAE featuring Tom Cruise, when advertisements appeared for set decorators, stuntmen, photographers, make-up artists and production assistants.

Recently, there has been a move to form an association of AGCC film makers who would show their movies at regional film festivals. The first ever regional film festival in Muscat was held in Oman in 2001.

Manufacturing Industries

Steel The UAE has a small but regionally significant steel industry. There are plants and facilities in Dubai, Sharjah and Abu Dhabi. Steel Makers Gulf Inc, located in the Jebel Ali Free Zone in the Emirate of Dubai, produces steel billets, bars and other structural steel products. Sharjah's Shattaf Anand Steel operate three steel rolling mills.

In Abu Dhabi, the government-owned General Industry Corporation opened a steel rolling mill and built a reinforced steel plant in the Mussafah industrial area in 2001. This plant has smelting and desalination facilities to help process the imported raw material. A private company, Abu Dhabi National Industrial Projects, formed in 1997, has established a joint venture with a German company to manufacture steel wire and rods. The manufacturing facility has been built in the Jebel Ali Free Zone in the Emirate of Dubai. It is yet another project that has lessened the UAE's dependence on imports.

Aluminium The government-owned Dubai Aluminium Company (Dubal), which was established in 1975, is one of the world's most energy-efficient industrial operations. It has one of the biggest stand-alone smelting complexes in the world. Raw material is imported from overseas. The major markets for Dubal's products are Japan, Iran, Korea and the US. A feature of its efficiency is the use of waste heat-conserving energy and water. Dubal has over 2000 employees.

To complement the smelting complex, Dubai Investments announced plans to start work on an aluminium rolling mill that will produce aluminium foil. Aluminium products actually made and marketed in the UAE include sheds, doors and water tanks.

Selling Sand to the UAE
An Australian company has been selling pink garnet sands to the structural steel works at Jebel Ali. The sand is used to clean the steel.

Cables High voltage cables are manufactured and exported from Jebel Ali Free Zone in Dubai. The Dubai Cable Company is a joint venture whose partners include the UK-based BICC (30%) and the emirate governments of Abu Dhabi and Dubai (35% each). In 1999, it undertook a significant expansion plan to install the most up-to-date computer controlled extrusion line to manufacture high voltage cables for the domestic and AGCC markets.

Other industries There is a developing household equipment industry. Tajer Glass Factory, in the Jebel Ali Free Zone in Dubai, has another factory in Ras al Khaimah. In 1999, a second glass company, Al Manal, also opened a factory in Ras al Khaimah.

The Abu Dhabi Flour and Fodder Mill expanded its capacity in 1999 with increased silo storage, the construction of a new mill and new equipment that will facilitate the faster discharge of grain.

The UAE Offset Group was responsibile for sewing up a deal to manufacture and export fire-fighting equipment. UTS-Burnstop LLC is a joint venture company whose partners are the UAE-based United Technical Services (51%), Burnstop Ltd from Finland (40%), and Dassault Investments (9%). The company's administrative office is in Abu Dhabi, and the manufacturing facility is in the Mussafah Industrial Zone. In addition to supplying the UAE market, products are exported to Asia, Europe and the Middle East.

In another Offset project, the National Cooling Company constructed cooling plants at Zayed Military City, Sweiham, in the Emirate of Abu Dhabi. These supply chilled water to buildings within a 15-kilometre distance of its radius. Tabreed also has operations in Al Ain in the Emirate of Abu Dhabi, and in the Emirates of Dubai and Ras al Khaimah.

> **Trade Follows Aid**
> In 1999, following the massive repression and expulsion of Albanian Muslims living in Kosovo, the UAE Red Crescent Society, after consulting the International Committee of the Red Cross, established a well provisioned refugee camp in Kukes, Albania. This later led to a joint venture between Normans of Albania and the Abu Dhabi-based Sahari Group to construct a magnesium alloy plant. Each has 50% equity in a smelter built at the Hamriyyah Free Zone in the Emirate of Sharjah. The raw magnesium is sourced from mines in Albania, and magnesium alloy is exported to Europe, Japan and the US.

A paper mill, producing fine paper rolls of all specifications and weights, was established in 2000. The fine paper products are marketed in the UAE and AGCC countries.

Dubai has a significant plastic plant, Union Plastics, located at Rashidiya. It supplies the UAE and AGCC countries.

International consumer goods are produced in the UAE.

Other products manufactured in the UAE include paint, foam, paper bags, ball point pens, aluminium sheets, wood panels, medical equipment, carpets and tissue paper.

There are more than 2000 factories in the UAE. This figure is growing at a rate of 15% per annum.

Consumer Goods

An increasing number of consumer goods in the supermarket, pharmacy or the souq is actually produced in the UAE as part of an import replacement programme. Consumer products made in the UAE include ice cream, cooking oil, nuts and crisps. The Emirate Macaroni Company produces several thousand tonnes of pasta per year. Dairies, including Marmum Dairy Farm Company, produce fresh milk, yoghurt, cheese and a thick creamy curd called *labneh*. The Marmum Dairy Farm Company also produces fruit juices under licence from Florida's Natural Growers.

The Al Khayam Group, whose products include Arabic sandwiches, hamburger breads, finger rolls, cakes and biscuits, opened a bakery in Dubai in 2001. It has been operating in Abu Dhabi for some years and plans to have retail outlets in Dubai, Sharjah, Ajman and Ras al Khaimah.

The Department of Agriculture and Animal Resources owns the Al Ain vegetable packaging factory in the Emirate of Abu Dhabi. The factory produces pickled vegetables, frozen vegetables and tomato paste.

The Dubai Investment Company was established in 1996. It went into a joint venture with the Swiss-based CAM Group to build an edible oil plant. Edible Oils LLC and the Dubai Investment Company hold 70% of the equity. The CAM Group has the remaining 30% of the equity. Production has started and its seed crushing plant is the largest facility of its kind in the Middle East.

Julphar, the largest pharmaceutical company in the Gulf with overseas operations in Ecuador and Germany, exports over 90% of its output from its three plants in the Digdagga district of Ras al Khaimah.

The other major pharmaceutical player is Gulf Inject whose headquarters are in the Jebel Ali Free Zone in the Emirate of Dubai. Gulf Inject's major product line is intravenous solutions which it exports to 26 countries.

Non alcoholic beverages, including spring water, mineral water and branded soft drinks such as Pepsi Cola, are bottled in the UAE. Spring water is sourced from the Wurayya Spring near Khor Fakkan in the Emirate of Fujairah and the Hatta Spring in Dubai.

A payoff from government-sponsored projects to improve date palm cultivation has been the production of fructose. Concept Food Industries in the Jebel Ali Free Zone in the Emirate of Dubai, has developed a process to produce fructose from dates. Fructose is a sweetening ingredient for food and beverages. A by-product from the processing of fructose is a high protein animal feed.

The federal government is encouraging traditional handicrafts. These include weaving, *talli* work (a kind of braiding to decorate local costumes) and the plaiting of the date-palm fibres which are then sewn into mats, bowls and baskets.

Garments are also manufactured in the UAE. A major company, International Textile, is based in Ajman. The textile industry is one of the fastest growing industries, and export markets for garments have been established in Europe and the US. Future growth depends on the export market which, in turn, is restricted by US quotas and the lack of executives with the necessary international marketing skills currently provided by expatriates.

The Dubai Government is encouraging unemployed UAE nationals and housewives to establish micro businesses. The plan is to issue them with an *individual establishment trade licence* and market their products or services through special promotional shows or via the Internet.

Construction

The early 1990s saw considerable economic activity relating to the construction of hotels, commercial properties and housing. Based on the number of cranes, a visitor to the UAE would conclude that the construction industry is an expanding industry. Major construction projects completed by the beginning of the 21st century include the out-of-this-world Burj al Arab Hotel, the equally stunning Jumeirah Beach Hotel, the Free Zones and Shaikh Rashid Terminal at Dubai International Airport. There was also considerable activity in the construction of office blocks and residential property.

The industry is highly competitive with both UAE companies and overseas companies (with a UAE sponsor and partner) having a presence in the market. The chairman of the Al Habtoor Group, one of the major UAE construction firms, reported in January 2001 that, despite a high turnover, profits are small.

Construction is a key sector of the UAE economy.

Future growth is projected to come from the utilities and leisure development sectors, and projects associated with Abu Dhabi's oil and gas industry.

Foreigners are not allowed to own real estate in the UAE, but can own houses in a few small selected areas. The land is leased for 99 years.

Consultancy Services
Skilled professionals are in short supply in education, finance, engineering and management. Consultancy assignments are plentiful for these occupations. Most consultancy roles in the UAE are filled by expatriates.

Defence Equipment
In March 1999, Abu Dhabi hosted its biggest ever defence exhibition known as *IDEX*. Some 800 companies from 41 countries attended the exhibition.

The 1998 defence expenditure was nearly USD 5 billion. That translated to USD1,434 per capita. Amongst AGCC countries, the UAE had the third highest per capita expenditure after Saudi Arabia and Kuwait. In 1999, UAE troops deployed in Kosovo made up the biggest contingent of the KFOR force, after NATO. The UAE is less interested in purchasing military hardware such as tanks and warships, than in acquiring military software such as training, maintenance and high-tech military support systems.

Giat of France plans to supply the UAE military with tanks. McDonald Douglas plans to supply the UAE air force with F-16 fighter aircraft. The UAE navy is looking into purchasing eight ocean-going patrol boats and six small frigates

How the French Won Lucrative Defence Contracts
Although many arms sales are made through intermediaries, the French were able to secure significant orders for military aircraft and tanks through the French President negotiating directly with the President of the UAE.

The UAE Foreign Legion
Like the commercial labour force, the UAE armed forces is made up mainly of non UAE nationals.

The UAE does not like paying cash to overseas companies for its defence assets. Its Ministry of Defence has been focusing on creative ways to acquire military equipment, including a barter arrangement where arms dealers are paid in UAE government bonds.

The UAE has also been successful in establishing creative terms of trade for the purchase of defence assets. Under the Offset programme, overseas companies who have successfully received a contract for the supply of defence equipment must invest a portion of their profits in a joint venture project in the UAE. In the case of defence contracts worth USD10 million or more, 60% of the value of the contract must be reinvested in joint ventures in the UAE. Successful defence tenderers can have up to 49% equity in joint ventures. The controlling 51% interest must be owned by UAE nationals or UAE companies. Proceeds from other defence Offset programmes have gone into gas distribution, horticulture, fish farming and processing, and the manufacture of fire-fighting equipment.

The UAE has not always been able to acquire all the defence assets on its shopping list. The US has been holding up a 1998 order for F-16 aircraft because it does not want to release source codes that would enable the UAE to know the fire control systems of Israeli and US aircraft.

CHAPTER 6

Choosing a Business Partner

Overview

Choosing a UAE business partner is probably the most challenging decision you will have to make. You cannot expect your UAE national sponsor to be an equal partner. The role of your UAE partner is to facilitate the entry of your business into the country. Your UAE partner will view his role as one to share in the profits of your business, if any. He will not be interested in sharing your losses or in contributing capital.

Great care needs to be exercised in the appointment of an agent or master distributor because once the appointment is made, the business laws make it very difficult to change your distribution arrangements. Although the company that you choose as your

UAE business executives who are nationals always wear the national dress.

business partner will have at least 51% UAE equity, it is most unlikely that UAE nationals will be part of the management team —other than as managing director, whom you will need to pay a courtesy call on and talk business generalities. The three key factors to be considered when choosing a UAE business partner are:

- Territorial coverage
- The management team
- Commitment

Territorial Coverage

As the UAE market is small by international standards, an overseas company would ideally appoint a distributor either for the Middle East, or the Gulf. However, each country in the region mandates that the business must have a UAE partner holding a 51% interest in the joint venture. This necessitates a separate distributor for each Gulf state.

There are a few companies with a pan-Gulf marketing capability. These companies do not have a branch structure and may have a different name in each AGCC country. The common element is the same minority shareholder who is also responsible for managing the companies throughout the region. In many instances, the minority shareholder managing the companies in the region is a western offshore company (often a UK trading company).

For most companies, the key UAE markets are Dubai, Abu Dhabi and Sharjah in that order. When negotiating the appointment of an agent or master distributor, investigate the potential distributor's area coverage. In many instances, the agents or master distributors will probably have offices in one, two or maybe three emirates: which will most likely be Dubai, Abu Dhabi and Sharjah, in that order. If they do not have offices in these three emirates, they will appoint sub agents or distributors in the other emirates for your product as they believe that business networks are emirate-based, rather than nationally-based, that is a Sharjah-based distributor has a better opportunity of making a sale to a Sharjah retailer than a distributor from another emirate.

Some western expatriate executives believe that it is better to have a different distributor in each emirate in case things do not work out with one distributor.

It is also difficult to find a company with a presence in all the emirates of the UAE. Organisations that have a presence throughout the UAE are usually companies which started off as British trading companies with a minority shareholding in a company in each of the emirates, and negotiating a contract to manage the companies.

You will usually need a UAE stakeholder in the emirate in which you choose to market your product or services, in order to attract UAE customers. Thus, if your business is in the Emirate of Abu Dhabi and your customer is the UAE national, you will need an Abu Dhabi partner as stakeholder or sponsor to secure business.

The Management Team

The composition of the management team has changed over the last decade. Previously, the non executive directors of large companies were usually UAE nationals; executive directors and senior management staff were usually British or American expatriates while the junior and supervisory ranks were usually filled by expatriates from the subcontinent. Smaller UAE companies often recruited non Gulf Arabs from Palestine, Egypt and Lebanon to fill their management and supervisory positions.

Today, non executive directors of large companies are usually UAE nationals or members of the royal families who sometimes take on the chairmanship of the companies. Subcontinent expatriates and UAE nationals have also moved into more senior management positions as executive directors and general managers. The UAE has also looked to countries such as Australia to source managers and other professionals.

Somewhat interestingly, Emirates Airlines has recruited 57 captains, 22 first officers and 300 cabin crew from Australia.

Expatriates from the subcontinent still make up most of middle management and junior management ranks in most companies. They are increasingly joined by western expatriates, especially from South Africa and New Zealand. A high proportion of executives working in specialist areas such as finance and information technology are from the sub-continent.

Many exporters believe that where a UAE business employs western and subcontinent expatriates, business objectives and strategies are understood and achieved better.

Western expatriates will find a cultural barrier where subcontinent expatriates need to get to know them before valuing their judgement. Marketing culture is different from the west. UAE distribution companies are not brand builders. They focus on price rather than brand.

In the unlikely event that the company marketing your product or service is actually managed by UAE nationals, you will find that most of the managers are related to each other as family is the first choice of business employees for UAE nationals. A common comment is that UAE nationals in supervisory and middle management positions do not have the same work ethic as expatriates.

Apart from the larger corporations, many UAE companies do not value feedback from their employees, nor engage in on-going training programmes. The Arab way of thinking is that the employee is the hired help; he is paid for a specific skill, and if he doesn't deliver, he is fired. There is limited social mobility for most of the expatriate work force as they are usually employed for a specific job.

Commitment

In evaluating a potential UAE business partner, check the company's current portfolio of products. If the company is large and looks efficient, it is likely to be already marketing products with brand names that are internationally well known. You will need to negotiate with the potential business partner, who will be your commercial agent, as to what energy levels will be spent on your brand and where your product or brand will be positioned in their portfolio.

Business Arrangements

UAE Exclusivity
The UAE welcomes foreign investment. However, since the laws relating to foreign investment are continually evolving and being modified, it is best to seek professional advice before entering the market.

Some business activities are the exclusive domain of UAE companies and no foreign ownership is permitted. Areas of business that overseas companies may not engage in include domestic banking, money investment and commercial agencies.

Appointment of a Distributor or Commercial Agent
There are a number of ways to establish a presence in the UAE. If your company is marketing a physical product to be imported into the UAE, the first step is to appoint a master distributor for all of the UAE or a distributor for each emirate. Where a number of distributors are appointed, each distributor in the UAE is usually given exclusivity for a specific product or a geographical area—usually a specific emirate. The law requires a commercial agents agreement when you appoint distributor.

Resident in the UAE under the Distributor's Umbrella
A second stage of business development is to locate an executive in the UAE without the problems of establishing a company. To locate in the UAE, you must have a sponsor. The easiest person to sponsor you is your own distributor. Under this arrangement,

while the distributing company works for the principal, visa paperwork shows the principal working for the distributor.

> **How a Well Known International Company Established its Office in the UAE**
>
> Before the opening of his regional office in the UAE, the general manager-designate of a major beverage company had visited the Middle East on numerous occasions. He was familiar with the business environment and had an excellent rapport with the executives of the UAE commercial agent and master distributor. Having advised their senior management of his intention to open an office, he and his family relocated to the UAE on a visitor's visa sponsored by the distributor. To obtain a work and resident visa, the general manager had to be an employee of a UAE registered company or locate in a free trade zone. He persuaded the distributor to engage him. The financial arrangements were that he would work theoretically *pro bono* for the distributor and receive sufficient funds from his company to allow him to live at the appropriate executive level. The distributor had many business units and the general manager was able to secure office accommodation away from the division that was responsible for distributing his products. In this way, he could be seen to be independent from his distributor.

Investors

The Federal Agency Law requires overseas companies or investors who want to market their product or service in the UAE to use the services of a UAE national or a UAE organization. Most businesses in the UAE must be at least 51% UAE nationally-owned. There are some exceptions. Businesses locating in the free trade zones can have 100% foreign ownership. In some of the technology parks, foreign ownership can be as high as 75%.

Technically, the foreign minority interests of a joint venture company can be expropriated by the majority UAE partner or the government. In the unlikely event of this happening, there are no specific rules for compensation. In practice, the authorities have never expropriated and would never do so, unless there is a compelling reason or public need to do so. If this were to occur, compensation would be generous.

An interesting situation arises when a multinational corporation (MNC) wants to market and have a presence throughout the UAE but cannot find a local company with a pan-UAE marketing capability. A solution to the problem is for the MNC to enter into a business arrangement with a number of UAE companies each with their strength in a specific emirate. As required by the law, 51% or more of the shares in the joint venture companies must be owned by UAE interests.

To exercise some direction over the joint venture company, the MNC will usually require some seats on the board. UAE business law requires the chairman of all joint ventures to be a UAE national as are most of the non-executive directors. The MNC is usually given the right to nominate the deputy chairman and it is nearly always mutually agreed that the managing director and most of the executive directors should be nominations of the MNC. The managing director and the senior management have historically been western expatriates or non Gulf Arabs but the situation is changing.

In joint ventures of this kind, there may be an arrangement where the MNC not only provides most of the executive directors and the senior management but also receives a management fee for the expertise it brings to the organisation. In addition to the management fee, the MNC may receive an additional bonus based on agreed financial performance indices.

Overseas companies can establish a branch office in the UAE but they must engage a UAE owned service company or a UAE national as a service agent. The principal role of the service company or service agent is to act as sponsor for the overseas branch office.

As a result of overseas companies needing to be sponsored and only being allowed 49% equity in joint ventures, the way that overseas companies establish themselves in each emirate can vary. In one emirate, the overseas company may enter into a joint venture with a UAE company whereas in another emirate, it may open a branch office and engage a UAE service company.

An overseas company that the authors had business dealings with, formed a joint venture in Abu Dhabi and operated a branch office in Dubai where it engaged a UAE service company as a sponsor. The company had retail outlets in Abu Dhabi, Dubai and Sharjah. The Sharjah outlet was a branch of the Dubai joint venture. The chairman and non-executive directors of the Abu Dhabi joint venture company were UAE nationals whereas in Dubai, there were no directors as the entity was a branch office with British senior management staff. The company had a management contract and their senior executive based in Dubai had pan-Gulf responsibilities. Its three core activities were trading, consumer products and the distribution of alcoholic beverages. A general manager based in Dubai headed the trading and consumer products divisions. As a result of complex alcoholic beverage regulations in the emirates, the beverage division appointed a general manager for Abu Dhabi and a general manager for Dubai, with responsibility for alcoholic beverage operations in Sharjah. The name of the local joint venture partner was included in the trading name of the company in Abu Dhabi but not in Dubai.

If you cannot find a sponsor, the chambers of commerce in each emirate may be able to help. Depending on the nature of your business, they may even be willing to act as your sponsor. There are two exceptions where sponsorship is not required. In the Emirate of Dubai, under local order 63 of 1991, professionals and those engaged in handicrafts are exempt. Some western expatriate lawyers and accountants practise in Dubai without a sponsor. The disadvantage is that they are unlikely to have UAE nationals among their clientele.

A sponsor is also not required if you locate in one of the free trade zones in the UAE. The disadvantage is that you will not enjoy the duty free import status for your exports to other AGCC countries.

Branch and Representative Offices

Companies marketing physical products or services, in the UAE can open a branch or representative office. Article 313 of the Company Law permits an overseas company to open a branch or representative office in the UAE. The law distinguishes between branch offices and representative offices. According to UAE business law, a company that opens a branch office can undertake business activities for which the branch office is licensed whereas a representative office can only promote the business of the parent company but cannot directly transact with customers or consumers. The opening of a branch office or representative office still needs the involvement of UAE nationals or UAE companies. In the case of a representative office, a UAE service agent must be appointed. The role of the service agent is to facilitate the acquisition of a resident visa for foreigners managing the branch office, and a trading licence to allow the company to function. The service agent also deals with the government, on behalf of the branch office, with respect to submitting tenders to the government and notifying the company of government regulations affecting business.

Joint Ventures

Many overseas companies enter into joint ventures with UAE nationals to form joint venture limited liability companies (LLC). In this structure, there needs to be a minimum of two shareholders and not more than 50 shareholders. There are certain minimum share capital provisions; in the case of Dubai, it is UAD 300,000. What overseas companies find attractive about LLCs is that shares are not open for public subscription and profits can be distributed on agreed ratios based on the contribution of the overseas companies in terms of management and technology.

Overseas companies cannot own more than 49% of the shareholding in LLCs. They can participate in a public shareholding company where the shares are open for public subscription but there are certain capital requirements. In 2001, the capital requirement was UAD 10 million. The disadvantage is that the overseas company can only take up 49% of the equity; the majority of the board and the chairman must be UAE nationals although the deputy chairman need not be a UAE national.

A variation is the private shareholding company. Like the public shareholding company, it issues shares but not through public subscription. The minimum capital required to form a private shareholding company was UAD 2 million, in 2001.

For overseas companies wanting to undertake a specific project, the formation of a joint venture consortium company may be the most suitable enterprise. Such joint ventures are known as *clandestine* companies. The existence of a clandestine company is only known to its partners and those contracting with it. Clandestine companies do not have to be registered or published in the ministry bulletins as the licence of the UAE partner will suffice. The UAE partner must have 51% of the equity but like the LLC, profits are distributed according to agreed ratios and factors like the company's contribution of technological know-how and management skills.

Dubai's local order 63 of 1991 permits non UAE nationals to form companies in certain business service areas, such as accountancy, without the need to have UAE nationals as partners. They must, however, engage a UAE national or a UAE company as a service agent.

You can also locate in a free trade zone. Here, sponsorship by a UAE company and a government business licence are not required. 100% foreign ownership of the business is allowed.

Partnerships

The UAE also permits overseas enterprises to trade in the UAE as partnerships. The law allows up to fifty partners. The disadvantage of partnerships is that the UAE partners must participate in the management of the company and share profits according to the capital formation.

Small to medium-sized companies which want to establish joint ventures should be aware that the UAE company will generally want you to contribute most of the capital, take most of the risk and manage the joint venture. The UAE company will expect to share in at least half of the profits.

Sponsorship and Ownership

All non UAE nationals who want to work in the UAE must have a sponsor in order to obtain a work visa and a residence permit. In many instances, under a system known as *kifala*, local companies ask UAE nationals to sponsor unskilled workers, who are usually from the subcontinent, for a fee.

Wives and dependants are normally on the husband's visa. An expatriate who has a resident visa can sponsor his wife and children. However, once the son turns 18 years of age, he can no longer be sponsored.

> **How to Obtain Permanent Residency for Your Family**
> This is fairly simple. First, get a sponsor so that you qualify for permanent residency (not so simple). Once you have permanent residency, you are allowed to sponsor your family and they will be entitled to permanent residency.

With permanent residency status, your wife or adult daughter can obtain a labour card. An expatriate wife needs a sponsor in order to obtain a work permit and a job. This is fairly easily obtained since a husband can sponsor his wife and children if he meets legal requirements with regard to salary and accommodation.

Expatriate fathers cannot sponsor their sons when their sons reach eighteen. The Ministry of Labour and Social Affairs has substantially increased the fees for labour cards from UAD 800 to UAD 2,000 for wives and daughters sponsored by their husbands or fathers. Concurrent with the increased labour card fees is a reduction in the sponsorship transfer fee from UAD 1,000 to UAD 500. This reduction is aimed at encouraging companies to recruit new employees from the significant number of unemployed or under-employed expatriates mainly from the subcontinent. In certain job categories sponsorship transfer fees have been abolished.

The change in fees is all part of the government's plan to regulate the labour market.

It is an offence for an expatriate to work for an employer other than the original sponsor. This usually carries a jail sentence of two months.

From time to time, bogus companies are established with the objective of illegally obtaining resident visas for "company employees". The Department of Naturalisation and Immigration of the Emirate of Ras al Khaimah dealt with the problem of a recent spate of illegal companies by insisting that companies requesting resident visas produce their trade licence in its original form. Any tampering to the trade licence, such as changing validity date, is subject to heavy fines. The government also looks at the tenancy contract and meets with the landlord or real estate agent to ensure that the premises are set up for busines purposes.

Expatriate executives are normally granted a five-year employment visa. Once settled in the UAE, it is difficult to change jobs as the law requires employees who are not UAE nationals to leave the country for six months before they can re-enter with a new sponsor. Expatriate employees must leave on good terms with their employer. If a complaint is made by your employer to the Labour Department, your passport could be stamped with a ban for one year. Curiously, even if your passport is stamped with a ban for one year, you are allowed to visit the UAE during that period but may not to take up employment.

If you wish to change your job, you must obtain a "no objection" certificate from your original sponsor. This condition does not apply if you can produce your university certificate in its original form.

An employer cannot vary the employment contract except by mutual consent. This means that the employer cannot reduce the employee's salary or vary the conditions of employment. If this does occur, the employee can quit without notice and receive all his benefits in accordance with Article 121 of the Labour Law. In the case of a company not honouring its contract, the employee can make a report to the Labour Department and have his sponsorship transferred to another company.

Employment contracts can be of two types: a limited period contract, or an unlimited period contract. If your employment contract is for an unlimited period and you have a manager's work visa, then you can terminate your employment after one month's notice. In changing employers you need to check that your employment contract does not contain a provision that precludes you from joining a competitive business.

Technically, the UAE sponsors hold the passport of the persons they sponsor. In reality, the sponsor does not hold the passport of executives who need to travel but does hold the passport of employees who are not of managerial status and do not travel.

UAE nationals who are directors of joint venture companies can require expatriates to seek their permission should they need to leave the UAE temporarily. It has been the authors' experience that expatriates, as a matter of courtesy, informally advise the chairman of their joint venture of any travel plans.

> **When Visiting the UAE, Make Sure Your Sponsor has Your Precise Details**
>
> On one of the many business trips that the authors made to the UAE, they flew first class on Gulf Air from the Sultanate of Oman (another AGCC country) and anticipated a breeze through immigration and customs as they were first off the aircraft. This was not the case.
>
> The usual practice when visiting the UAE on a regular basis, if you are a senior executive, is to give your passport details to a member of the UAE joint venture company who will also be an expatriate executive. He, in turn, will pass them on to a middle level executive who specialises in business travel and who takes care of the details and arrangements. Unfortunately, a mistake was made in the authors' nationality; they were described as Austrian rather than Australian. This caused a considerable delay at the airport but eventually they were allowed through.

Senior expatriates and their families normally reside in the UAE but expatriates who earn less than UAD 3,000 a month cannot sponsor their spouse or children.

Commercial Agency Law Number 18

Law number 18 of 1981 requires an overseas company which wants to market its products in the UAE to appoint a commercial agent. It is important to brief your legal advisor that the term *commercial agent*, under law number 18, is not the same as a commercial agent as defined in the civil transaction code and commercial transaction law. Under Commercial Agency Law Number 18, the commercial agent is a merchant conducting his activities independent of the principal conducting his business in his own name, and cannot bind the principal to the commercial agent's transaction. This is not the case with the appointment of a commercial agent under the civil transaction code and commercial transaction law. If you appoint a distributor under the civil transaction code and the commercial transaction law, the principal (that is the overseas company) will be bound by the actions of its distributor. In appointing a distributor, make sure that the appointment is made under the Commercial Agency Law.

After the agreement is made, it must be registered with the Ministry of Economy and Commerce. According to UAE law, there must be exclusivity with the distributor. If the distributor is a corporate body, a majority of the partners or shareholders must be UAE nationals.

The legal agreement can only be terminated if the Ministry of Economy and Commerce removes it from the commercial agency register. The Ministry of Economy and Commerce will only consider cancelling the agreement if there is mutual agreement between the principal (that is the overseas company) and the distributor. Even where there is mutual agreement between the overseas company and the UAE distributor, the Ministry may not terminate the arrangement if it considers that there is not a good enough reason.

CHAPTER 7

Business Culture

Overview
Arabs are no more a single homogeneous group than are Europeans. The business culture of the UAE is full of conundrums and pragmatic interpretations of the law. For example, gambling is prohibited but none the less there are slot machines at the Seafarers Club, a rest and recreation facility used by sailors from the US navy. Similarly, there is no gambling at the horse races but there are intelligence games.

> **How to Play Intelligence Games**
> At the horse races in Dubai, like anywhere else in the world, there is a race guide that tells you about the horses, the jockeys and the times of the races. There are no bookmakers at the race track and gambling is not allowed. Intelligence games are. To play an intelligence game, you fill out a form in the race guide and try to pick the winner of each race. If you are intelligent enough to pick which horse will come in first, second and third in all the races, you have the opportunity to win a substantial prize.

Business and Religion
The UAE is a Muslim country where religion permeates everyday life and codes of conduct for business.

The business culture of the UAE is linked to Islam. It is seen in everyday speech where, when confirming an upcoming meeting with UAE nationals, they are likely to respond with the word *inshallah*, literally meaning, if God is willing. The use of the word *inshallah* may also be a reflection of the more laid-back style of business practised by UAE nationals.

> ### The Friday Weekend
> Friday is the Holy Day of the Muslim week. For most expatriates working in the UAE, the weekend starts on Thursday afternoon and people return to work on Saturday morning.
>
> ### The Koran and Interest Rates
> The literal interpretation of the Koran forbids the charging of usury. However, UAE banks do charge interest on loans. The modern interpretation is that excessive interest rates should not be charged.
>
> ### The Case of the Abu Dhabi Islamic Bank
> The Abu Dhabi Islamic Bank has become the largest Islamic bank in the world. What makes it different from other commercial banks is that it has a social as well as business agenda, and its professional banking staff has a thorough knowledge of Islamic principles. In banking, this means that the bank's business activities conform strictly with Islamic principles.

Similarly, when bidding farewell, a UAE national may say *fee man allah*, which literally means, may God go with you. Muslims are expected to pray five times a day: at dawn, noon, afternoon, dusk and at night. It is not uncommon for UAE business people to stop work or interrupt their business meeting in order to pray.

When visiting the UAE on business, avoid the topic of religion and do not walk in front of people when they are praying.

Islamic thinking is influenced by the concept of *shuras*, that is extensive consultation. This includes decision-making at management levels. The word *shuras* can broadly be translated as "teams at all levels of society". It is quite similar to the Japanese *ringi* system where teams at all levels of management approve or disapprove management decisions. The concept of *shuras* is not democracy, but the suggestion is that, like a modern management

The famous mosque at Jumeirah is a landmark in Dubai and the huge stone structure is a classic example of modern Islamic architecture.

team, consensus is better than voting or having a boss that directs what is to be done.

All Muslims try to make a pilgrimage to Mecca, known as the Hajj. Management must give leave to any Muslim employee wanting to go on the Hajj.

Maintaining Islamic Traditions in Business
The UAE government has a programme to ensure that, by 2020, 90% of teachers will be UAE nationals. The government's objective is to ensure the continuance of Islamic traditions. Presumably, new graduates will reinforce Islamic traditions when they enter the work force.

The Koran and Agri Business
Farmers in the UAE destroy their sheep when they show signs of illness, rather than use modern farming techniques like drenching as a preventive measure. This is because a modern interpretation of the Koran, the Muslim Holy Book, prohibits drenching and the general use of chemicals.

Ramadan

Ramadan falls on the ninth month of the Muslim year. The Muslim year follows the lunar calendar so that Ramadan falls at a different month in the Gregorian calendar, each year. During Ramadan, there is no eating or drinking from dawn to dusk and non Muslims are expected to respect these Islamic rites.

For expatriates, this means no business lunches, no coffee or tea breaks and no smoking in the office. Despite the restrictions, there is a certain degree of leniency for people who are not Muslims. For example, in Dubai, the most cosmopolitan city in the UAE, the five-star hotels will serve food and alcohol during the day if it is consumed in your room.

Boosting Sales During Ramadan
Prior to Ramadan, Muslims go on a shopping spree for food as fasting from dawn to dusk during Ramadan makes them too tired to do grocery shopping during the day. A marketer of canned fruits was able to persuade Muslim customers to stock up on his products and to consume them at the two meals that occur between dusk and dawn. During Ramadan, the evening meal is called *iftar* and the late supper or very early breakfast is known as *suhur*. He convinced Muslim customers that the fructose and other added sugars in the canned fruits would quickly restore energy levels at the *iftar* meal, and be a source of energy for the next day when consumed at the *suhur* meal.

Women in Business

Although most women UAE nationals wear black *abayas* (a form of loose long coat) and give the overt appearance of being chaperoned, some work in organisations such as the UAE military.

This bank is for women customers only.

> **The President's View**
> According to UAE President Shaikh Zayed, women have the right to work everywhere. Islam accords women their rightful status and encourages them to work in all sections as long as they are given the appropriate respect. The president has said that the basic role of women is to bring up children but, over and above that, opportunities must be offered to a woman who chooses to perform other functions.

Women do not generally have a high profile in business in the UAE but conditions are changing. In 1999, there were more women attending university in the UAE than men. An explanation for this is that more UAE men attend overseas universities than women, and many men choose to enter the work force after completing secondary school. Anecdotal evidence suggests the number of women in the work force has doubled in the last 20 years.

A 2001 report published by the office of the wife of the president of the UAE, who is also the chairperson of the UAE Women's Federation, stated that only 18% of women UAE nationals are employed.

UAE women prefer to work for the federal government. In 2000, nearly 60% of federal civil servants were women. Somewhat surprisingly, less than 10% of municipal civil servants were women.

Although UAE women and, in particular, UAE women graduates want to work, they are selective job seekers. They have a particular aversion to working in business and this might explain why 80% of UAE nationals seeking a job through the Ministry of Labour and Social Affairs are women.

> **UAE Women Say No to Corporate Careers**
> A 1999 study entitled, *Attitudes to the Private Sector*, whose respondents were students at Abu Dhabi's Women's Higher College of Technology found that:
> - 97% of women wanted to work after graduation
> - 40% wanted to work in the oil sector where the principal shareholder is the government
> - 48% wanted to work in government
> - a low 12% wanted to work in the private sector
>
> Reasons cited for not wanting to work in the private sector were:
> - higher salaries in the civil service and the government owned oil companies
> - greater benefits in these two sectors
> - job security in these two sectors
> - shorter working hours in these two sectors

Whereas a corporate culture of gender equality exists in the west with women crashing through the glass ceiling, no such culture exists in the UAE although Dubai has one of the most liberal corporate gender regimes. Women in the UAE do work for corporations but they are often found in banking where business dealings are only with women.

> **Teaching UAE Women to Smile**
> UAE women do not smile in public as it is considered lewd behaviour. The Emirate of Dubai, which sees tourism as a high growth business and a source of employment for UAE women graduates in customer service roles, is training women for these roles. Its Department of Tourism and Commerce Marketing has had to explain to UAE women that it is acceptable, indeed desirable and part of their job, to smile when dealing with tourists from the west.

You will never lose your way to the ladies' washroom.

It is relatively easy for western expatriate wives to find jobs as personal assistants, teachers and nurses. This is because their husbands are usually on two to five-year management assignments. They will, however, be employed on local rather than expatriate conditions and will not enjoy the fringe benefits of a housing allowance, company car and home paid leave. A good source for looking for work is the country's diplomatic mission or chamber of commerce. There are also a number of recruitment agencies that can be approached.

Don't Forget to Get Your Husband's Permission If You Want a Job
Yes, that's true! To the amazement of many an expatriate wife, the prospective employer will require a "no objection" letter signed by the husband before any wife is offered a job.

Business Transactions

In the UAE, business meetings can be formal or informal. An informal meeting takes place in an office, usually one on one, without a formal agenda. In a meeting, telephone calls will not be held and there will be frequent interruptions.

> **Telephone Etiquette**
> When a call comes in, it is always taken. A former diplomat who returned to work in the UAE said, *"You will find your meeting interrupted by phone calls—these are always taken as no one returns a call here."*

Another surprise is to find yourself in an office with other business visitors, all having the same appointment time but with different agendas.

The formal meeting will probably be in the board room with a number of executives. Managers and government officials who are UAE nationals like to attend formal business meetings in groups of about five people. There is often a formal agenda and there may be a formal presentation. The level of presentation can range from a sophisticated power point presentation, in the case of larger companies, to an informal report delivered orally. At the meeting, the most senior executive or official will normally sit at one end of the board table. If you are a senior executive, you will be invited to sit on the right of the most senior executive or government official.

Although there can be a formal agenda, it may not be adhered to and discussions can be wide-ranging. Frequent business travellers make reference to the agenda being *grazed* rather than slavishly followed.

As most managers in the UAE are expatriates, the manner in which your transactions are conducted will depend on the nationality of the manager you are transacting with. Negotiations with western expatriates are direct from the start. Managers who are UAE nationals, and Asian and subcontinent expatriates will spend some time getting to know you and exchanging pleasantries. It may take up to two or three visits, before full and frank discussions can be made.

Nepotism is part of the culture in businesses owned and managed by UAE nationals. The most senior member of the family will almost always get the top job, regardless of ability..

If you are transacting with a subcontinent expatriate in a small or medium-sized company where all the directors are UAE nationals, you may find some indecision as the directors are less willing to empower their managers.

Patience is required when dealing with managers who are UAE nationals. UAE nationals do not manage time with the same enthusiasm found in most countries in the west. What you will find different in dealing with UAE nationals is the *inshallah* mentality, where appointments and schedules are not rigidly kept. In fact, constantly checking your watch at a business meeting to move things along may be interpreted as a sign of rudeness. Executives and government officials who are UAE nationals have difficulty managing time because their priorities are different. Whereas, for example, the Japanese executive puts business before family, it is the other way around for UAE nationals. Meetings get behind schedule because UAE nationals attend to family affairs first and business second. Senior managers and government officials may not be able to attend meetings on time as they can be called away by a member of the royal family.

English is the language of business in the UAE even though the national language is Gulf Arabic. This is a dialect of classical Arabic.

You will find that your business dealings in the UAE will be with managers (almost always men) who are sophisticated and who have a good grasp of international business. This is not so surprising (there are differences in each emirate) as most executives are expatriates and the economy is built on exports and imports.

When transacting with smaller businesses, make sure there is a clear understanding of the terms of trade. Small to medium-sized businesses do not always appreciate the subtle distinction of international trade terms like selling free alongside ship (FAS), as distinct from selling free on board (FOB).

Check the Fine Print in Your Letter of Credit

An Australian company exporting feed stock negotiated a deal with a UAE trader. Among the terms of trade mutually agreed to was a letter of credit, with payment due 60 days after the stock feed had been shipped from the Australian port. Despite this provision being expressly written into the letter of credit, the trader chose to interpret the terms of trade as payment sixty days after the arrival of the stock feed in the UAE. As it was an international letter of credit, the Australian exporter was guaranteed payment by the bank but not as originally scheduled, and not in accordance with the provisions of the letter of credit.

Business people planning to transact with smaller UAE businesses should be aware that they may not always know the trade terms of the International Chamber of Commerce (INCO), such as C & F (where the exporter pays the shipping costs and freight) and CIF (where the exporter pays shipping costs, insurance and freight).

A Business Tip: Exercise Good Credit Control with Customers

According to an *Economist* report in 1997, less than 1% of personal cheques were dishonoured in Europe. Not so in the UAE, where it has been reported that over 5% of personal cheques are dishonoured.

A possible explanation is that when UAE nationals pay by cheque, they forget that their cheque may not yet be presented. They continue to write cheques believing they have sufficient funds. It is probably for this reason that writing a dishonoured cheque is a criminal offence.

Souq fraud has become more frequent. This is a situation where fraudsters buy products at wholesale prices on credit using their trade licence, sell to consumers for cash at lower than recommended retail prices, and then flee the UAE without paying the distributor. Souq fraud can be suspected when, for example, a trade licence to purchase electronic products at wholesale prices is used to purchase building materials. A variation on this theme is an emerging trend for some trading companies to offer commissions to their sales people based on their purchases rather than on what they can sell to wholesalers and retailers. Trading companies invite trouble when they remunerate their sales people on purchases rather than sales.

> **The Magical Business Transaction**
> The magic of Aladdin and the genie in the bottle who can grant wishes is alive and well in the UAE. The subject of witchcraft in business came to a head in 2000 when a woman was charged in the *Shariah* religious court in Ras al Khaimah of casting a spell on her former husband and his sister. The court found the woman guilty and she received a sentence of four months in prison. The court further ruled that, in the future, anyone else convicted of casting a spell would be sentenced to death. There are two problems with this decision. The first is that many wealthy and educated UAE nationals use magic, or a genie, or *djinn* to resolve disputes. Secondly, the Koran mentions djinn 37 times and has a *sura* (chapter) devoted to the subject

There have been a number of cases where UAE nationals have been involved in magic to resolve disputes. In 1998, a senior executive with the Dubai Islamic Bank gave more than USD242 million to a Nigerian witch doctor as the UAE national was convinced that this was the only way he could break the spell cast on him.

Sales Forecasting
A visiting expatriate executive in agri-business made the observation that the outlook of UAE small businessmen, especially in farming, tend to be short-term. He found that if the UAE farmer feels that he can only sell ten sheep in the short term, that would be the size of his flock.

A Universal Wish
A business visitor to the UAE observed that almost all UAE nationals have the same wish—if they could proliferate the UAE with trees, the rains would come back to the desert.

When Words Fail You
The wife of a western expatriate regional manager took a pair of trousers to her Indian tailor and asked him to make a second pair exactly the same as the pair she left him. Sure enough, he did—right down to the hole in the original pair.

The Distributor's Dilemma
The vice president of a major beverage company, in his efforts to widen the distribution of his company's products, approached the Abu Dhabi National Hotels Corporation (ADNHC) which controlled 13 hotels and other outlets. The problem was that ADNHC wanted to buy directly from the major beverage company and not through its official UAE distributor. A particular legal difficulty was the commercial agency agreement giving exclusivity to the master distributor. The vice president solved the problem by supplying ADNHC direct, but paying the master distributor a fee based on the margin it would have made had it transacted directly with ADNHC.

UAE nationals will not directly say "no" to your business proposal, so you will need to read between the lines to know when "yes" means "yes" and when "yes" means "no". In a meeting with UAE nationals or Asian and subcontinent expatriates, you will be considered to have lost control if you become aggressive and bang your fist on the table, raise your voice or, even worse, lose your temper. It is also considered bad manners to beckon with the upright finger or to point with your index finger.

At a meeting with senior government officials or directors who are UAE nationals, it is better to err on the formal side and address them by their title. Say "minister" or "director general" if this is appropriate.

Frequent business travellers to the UAE often point out that concluding a deal is not so much a matter of time but timing. To a greater degree than in the west, mode, moment and place are most important. When you return to your home office, it is often a good idea to write a letter to the people you have met confirming the outcomes of your discussions.

As with all business transactions, choice of words is most important. When transacting with UAE nationals, communication should be more diplomatic and less direct and confrontational. When organising an important business meeting with senior UAE executives or government officials, keep in touch with all levels. Your personal assistant should keep in contact with the UAE ministry's personal assistant, and your other colleagues should keep in touch with their counterparts in the UAE.

When you have concluded a significant deal, don't expect a bottle of champagne to be opened in the office. It is illegal to have alcohol on office premises in the UAE.

Bending the Rules

There is no overt bribery in the UAE. In fact there is not much point in offering a bribe to UAE nationals as they have enough money anyway. A case was reported where the director of the new international airport in Dubai accepted a bribe. When this became known, the royal family demanded his immediate resignation. Although there is no bribery, there are *facilitation fees*. These are usually paid to low level civil servants, who are not UAE nationals, for small favours. The payment is made indirectly through a *Mr Fixit*.

> **Case 1**
> A regional manager had to submit the original certificate of his degree to the government in order to obtain his work visa. He could not as it was in a container together with his personal effects, in transit to the UAE. How did he solve the problem? He paid a facilitation fee to a non UAE government official through his company's Mr Fixit.
>
> **Case 2**
> A regional manager was relocating his office across town and wanted to retain his telephone number for continuity amongst his customers. The customer service supervisor said that was not possible. What did he do? He arranged for a facilitation fee to be paid to a supervisor in the utility company. The outcome was that he was able to retain the number.

Most UAE nationals are wealthy in their own right and would be hard to bribe. Bribery is most likely to occur amongst non Gulf Arabs, specifically Egyptians and Moroccans working as junior or middle level executives in the government or business. They are the most likely people to ask you for a gift (which is UAE code for a bribe).

While no tax is levied in the UAE, in reality, a certain amount of bribery goes on to enable the most mundane commercial transactions to occur. Bribery is particularly prevalent in the evaluation of bids and the award of contracts.

When public tenders are called for, the usual conditions include the issue of tender documents against a non refundable fee. The non refundable fee depends on the size of the project but can often be UAD 1,000 which must be paid by cash or a banker's order. The tenderer is then required to put up a bid bond equal to 5% of the tender value for a period of 90 days. The successful tenderer is then required to replace the bid bond with a performance bond equal to 10% of the contract value.

The UAE is a place where money can buy almost anything. Rumour has it that at one of the luxury hotels, a hugely wealthy guest requested a bath filled with goat's milk. For the appropriate fee, the request was fulfilled.

> **How to Use Regulations to Your Advantage**
> The purchase of alcoholic beverages for off premise consumption is strictly regulated in the UAE. A licence is required to purchase alcoholic beverages for off premise consumption. The number of such retail outlets is also strictly limited and the amount of alcohol that can be purchased is tied to the consumer's salary. Each time a consumer purchases an alcoholic beverage, the transaction is recorded in a kind of ration book. One enterprising supplier turned this into a loyalty marketing programme. Stamps in the ration book entitled the consumer to prizes such as tee-shirts, beach towels and umbrellas.

Bizarre Attractions

Many UAE nationals and expatriates leave the UAE during the blazing hot days of summer. Over the three months of July, August and September, there is a mass exodus of people. Expatriates and their families head for their homeland and UAE families escape to the more temperate climes of Europe and the Americas. To encourage residents to stay put, the Dubai government collaborates with the business sector to stage extraordinary events in July and August each year. The objective is to keep the wheels of business turning during the summer months.

Things Run Hot and Cold in Dubai
Some bizarre UAE attractions include:

Ice Sculptures
With an outside temperature of 40^0 C, miniature trains transport passengers around an indoor exhibition of ice sculptures.

The Ice Cream Cake
An ice cream cake which weighed four tonnes, and was the size of an Olympic swimming pool, was made to persuade UAE nationals to stay at home during summer rather than go abroad.

World's Longest Gold Chain
Dubai unveiled the longest ever gold chain at the 1999 Dubai Shopping Festival. South Africa's Anglo Gold Company, with the support of the World Gold Council, sponsored its making. Made of 22 carat gold, it measured 4.2 km when completed. At the end of the festival, about 10,000 people bought parts of the chain.

The Ice Hockey Rink
In Dubai there is an ice hockey rink that seats 1,500 people. It has corporate facilities, including dining rooms, as part of a strategy to develop lavish sporting facilities to eventually host the Olympic Games.

Dubai Shopping Festival
The Dubai Shopping Festival is a major event aimed at attracting visitors to Dubai. The event features Arab entertainment by leading Lebanese singers, international shows featuring cartoon characters, and an international fashion week. During the festival, each street is decorated to match a particular theme.

Expatriates normally return to the UAE in August. In many instances, their families remain for an extra month or so. This translates to a male oriented managerial population in pubs and clubs during the month of September.

A Privileged View for the Privileged Few

The Burj al Arab or Arab Tower, in English, is located on a man-made island off the coast of Dubai. The hotel, at 341 m, is as tall as the Eiffel Tower, and its sail shape is as graceful as Australia's Sydney Opera House. It is the tallest self contained hotel in the world and it dominates the shores of the Arabian Gulf. The Burj al Arab is owned by the royal family of Dubai and is meant to be a monument as well as a hotel.

The hotel markets itself as the world's only seven-star hotel and is unashamedly elitist. To stay at the Burj al Arab, you will have to break a very large piggy bank—it is an over the top super hotel with a view for the super rich few. If you are not a guest, it will cost you USD100 to stand in the foyer and gawk at the surrounds.

Features of the hotel include a royal suite and two presidential suites. The royal suite is a mini palace with 22 carat gold ceilings and a dining room with chairs covered in leopard skin. The bathroom is marble, and the bedroom features a revolving bed so that you can watch the TV from any angle. You can live in the 780 sq m royal suite for UAD 25,000 per night, as the Sultan of Brunei did. In fact, the Sultan of Brunei thought the Burj al Arab so good, he booked a further 50 suites for his entourage.

The Burj al Arab is rumoured to be featured in the next James Bond Film.

The duty free shops at Dubai airport are famous for their bargains and consumer premiums. How do they do it? The short answer is, if your company wants to distribute its products in downtown Dubai, you must supply the duty free airport shops at breakeven or very low margins. There is an on-going marketing programme to persuade travellers to buy at the Dubai duty free shops. In 2001, they ran a promotion, *The Two Most Tempting Prizes On Earth*. One prize was the chance for 5,000 travellers to win USD1,000,000 and become a Millennium Millionaire through purchasing a lottery ticket for USD278. The other prize was a

The out of this world Burj al Arab Hotel is a seven-star hotel.

luxury car which would be shipped to the winner's home free of charge. The price for this lottery ticket was USD139.

Business Greetings
Business greetings in the Arabic tend to be more formal and more drawn out. A typical greeting might be:

Greeter:	As'salam alaikoom (peace be upon you)
Response:	Wa alaikoom as'salam (and upon you peace)
Greeter:	Kif halak (how are you-*literally how is your colour*)
Response:	Zane (good) or Wajid zane (very good)
Greeter:	Al hamdu lilah (thank God for your safe arrival)

It is not the custom for women executives to shake hands with a male UAE national nor is it the custom for a male executive to shake the hands of a woman UAE national.

After the greetings, it is normal practice to exchange business cards. Business cards are not exchanged with the same formality as in Japan or Hong Kong.

Experienced international managers, when presented with a business card, usually leave the card on the board room table. If they are meeting a number of people, the cards are put on the table in the order of the people sitting opposite them.

When visiting the UAE, it is desirable but not mandatory to have the reverse side of the business card in Arabic. When meeting Arabic speaking directors or managers, the card should be presented with the Arabic print face up. It is the custom for UAE companies who have an association with a famous brand name, such as Pepsi Cola, to reflect the company name and the brand name on their business card. The decision to have Arabic on your business card really depends on whom you are transacting with. If your business dealings are with managers who speak English, there is no need to have Arabic on your business card.

UAE nationals in the business sector will most likely be directors of the company and will only want to talk generalities of your business. The detailed discussions will most likely be with the expatriate management team.

Business Hospitality

There is an Arab saying that "if there is not more than enough there is not enough". This reflects the importance of business hospitality in the UAE. At meetings, you will always be offered refreshments; most of the time it will be coffee. As an alternative to Arab coffee, you may be offered *chi suliman,* an Arab-style clear, sweet tea.

When One Cup of Coffee is Not Enough and More Than Two is Too Much

When you are offered Arab coffee at a business meeting, it is the custom to drink two cups. The reason is that if you drink only one cup, it signals that your hosts' coffee is not good. If you drink more than two cups, you are wearing out your welcome. After you have drunk your second cup, when a third cup is offered, shake your cup as a signal that you have had enough. If not, the server will refill your cup as he is under instruction to keep your cup full until you have signalled, by shaking your cup, that you have had enough.

In the UAE, you may be offered French, American, Turkish or Arab coffee. French coffee is in fact Nescafé (instant coffee), American coffee is percolated coffee, Turkish coffee is sweet and served in a small glass, and Arab coffee is the bitter Bedouin coffee containing cardamom and consumed from small cups without handles. Traditionally, Arab coffee is served from a large brass jug. In keeping with modern times, Arab coffee is now often served from a thermos flask which is a refined shape of the traditional brass jug. Dates will often be offered when you are served Arabic coffee. It is considered polite to accept the coffee even if it is not to your taste.

Most business meetings are conducted at restaurants or hotels with restaurants. It is very rare to be invited to an executive's home to meet his wife and family if they are UAE nationals. In the unlikely event that you are invited to a UAE national's home for a meal, you will probably find that the family eat together although the women will be grouped at one end. Extended families usually have a meal together on Friday, as western families have Sunday lunch together.

These days, western expatriates consume a lot less alcohol at business lunches than in the past. Subcontinent and Asian business executives generally do not consume alcohol at business lunches.

> **Entertaining UAE Nationals and Asian Expatriates**
> - Find out, discreetly, through their personal assistant how they would like to be entertained.
> - Inquire whether they would like to bring their wife, most will not.
> - If your guests do not consume alcohol, it is always a safe rule to follow suit.

At lunch, western expatriates will normally entertain you at the coffee shop of a five-star hotel or at their club for a light lunch. Dinner will normally be at a five-star hotel in the main dining room, where wine and other alcoholic beverages are served. Corporate business entertaining includes a "Bedouin feast" in the desert and corporate hospitality boxes at the horse races.

Other business entertainment venues include sporting clubs and functions sponsored by the foreign chambers of commerce. There are also business clubs centering on the World Trade Centre in Dubai. If you are entertaining UAE nationals, and you would like to consume an alcoholic beverage, it is considered good manners to ask before you order.

Somewhat surprisingly in a Muslim country, pork is available on hotel menus and at the supermarket. As with alcohol, it is not a good idea to order pork if you are dining with Muslims. Not all hotels have pork on their menus as a separate kitchen is needed with a separate preparation area and a refrigerator to keep the pork away from other meats.

Subcontinent expatriate managers generally entertain informally at lunch and dinner in free standing Lebanese restaurants. They will usually know the owner of the restaurant.

UAE nationals that you invite out for lunch or dinner, may decline to have more food out of politeness. Don't take them too literally; offer more food again. Curiously, although UAE nationals

The Jumeirah Beach Hotel is shaped like a wave.

and other Gulf Arabs are polite and hospitable when they order (say coffee) in a five-star hotel, they are not inclined to say "please" or "thank you" to the Filipina service staff.

When in the UAE, it is the custom that your business partner will pick up the tab for business entertainment except when it is at the hotel where you are staying. Similarly, when your UAE business partner visits you in your country, you will be expected to pick up the business entertainment tab unless it is at the hotel where the UAE visitor is staying.

Gift giving is not as widely practised in the UAE as it is in Japan. Occasions when you will usually receive a gift are on your first visit to the UAE, or if you are travelling with your wife or manager. If you are travelling with your wife or manager, it is good business manners to reciprocate the gesture. An item symbolic of your country is considered an appropriate gift.

> **Beware of the Sheep's Eye**
> It may still be possible that you get an invitation to a genuine Bedouin lunch or dinner. This will be held in a large tent in the desert. The meal will probably consist of roast goat and/or roast lamb/mutton and rice. Your Bedouin host will refer to the goat as *lham* (lamb) as all meat is *lham* in Arabic. There is usually no crockery, and it is the custom to sit in a circle and strip the carcass with your bare hands. A word of warning! Do not use your left hand. This is considered bad form as the left hand is used to perform ablutions.
>
> If you are an honoured guest, a treat is in store for you—you will be offered the sheep's or goat's eye. This is considered a great delicacy.

Corporate gift giving is part of business hospitality in the UAE. In most instances, gifts are usually modest such as ballpoint pens and diaries with your company logo. At more upmarket corporate functions attended by more senior managers, a more expensive gift, such as a watch with a company logo may be given.

Business Hours

The business week is usually from Saturday to midday on Thursday. The hours of business depend on the nature of the business. Noel Coward's famous line, "Mad dogs and Englishmen go out in the midday sun", does not apply in the UAE where retail trading hours are generally from 8:00 a.m. to 1:30 p.m. and in the afternoon from about 5:00 p.m. to 9:00 p.m. Government offices and banks usually open at around 7:00 a.m. and close for the day at around 1:00 p.m. The oil industry and many commercial enterprises are open from 8:00 a.m. to 5:00 p.m.

Executives working in western style corporations tend to work from about 8:00 a.m. until about 6:00 p.m. Non managerial employees normally work eight hours per day and 48 hours a week. Those employed in the hospitality and retail sectors normally work longer hours, often nine hours a day. Hours of work are reduced, usually two hours daily, during the holy month of Ramadan. An employee is entitled to 30 days' paid leave when he completes a year of service.

> **Adjusting the Weekend**
> Some western style corporations like to take as their weekend, Friday, the Muslim sabbath, and Saturday, which is usually a day off in most western countries. Emirates Airlines adopted the practice of a Friday/Saturday weekend but came under pressure from more conservative elements of the Muslim clergy to make the weekend Thursday/Friday. The mullahs believed that making Saturday a day of rest could be interpreted as the company acknowledging the Jewish sabbath.

From Saturdays to Wednesdays, government offices open between 7:00 a.m. and 7:30 a.m., and close for the day between 1:00 p.m. and 1:30 p.m. Banks open a little later, 8:00 a.m. or 8:30 a.m.

Business Dress

UAE nationals are encouraged to wear national dress by their rulers who set the example. This extends to those working in government and business. As there are styles in western dress, so are there styles in Arab dress. National dress for men consists of a *guttrah*, which is a piece of cloth worn on the head, and secured with a rope-like device known as an *egal*. The egal and the guttrah make up the head dress. In the early days, it was fairly easy to identify the country an Arab came from, by the colour of his guttrah. Traditionally, only Saudis and Jordanians wore red and white checked guttrahs. Today, Arabs other than Saudis and Jordanians also wear red and white guttrahs. The colour and style of the guttrah worn by a UAE national reflect his personal taste.

The long nightshirt worn by men is known as a *thobe* or *dishdasha*. In summer, UAE nationals wear white thobes or dishdashas; in winter the thobe or dishdasha is darker, with blue and grey being the popular colours, and made from heavier fabric. In winter, long trousers are worn under the thobe and a western style brand name jacket provides additional warmth. A longish tee-shirt or sarong-like garment worn under the thobe is a *wizar*.

On more formal occasions, and in the winter, a *bisht* or kind of academic gown is worn over the dishdasha. The colour of the bisht is dictated by fashion but is often black or brown. As with the thobe or dishdasha, the bisht worn in summer is of a lighter material than the winter bisht which is of a heavier material. The bisht is similar to the western dinner suits or tuxedos.

The slip on shoes that UAE nationals wear are always referred to as slippers.

Items of women's apparel include a *shallah*, which is a headscarf like the male guttrah, and an *abiyah*, which is a long, black, lightweight coat. Under the abiyah, women usually wear a *karetoora*, which is a very colourful dress. Younger women often wear designer denim jeans. It is the custom to buy new clothes at the end of Ramadan.

Expatriates and non UAE Arabs working in the banking and financial services, and the professions, are often found in suits even in summer when the temperature is more than $40°C$, as their offices and cars are airconditioned. Those in business and the civil service usually wear jackets in the winter, and a shirt and tie in the summer. The shirt is always long-sleeved and the skin is not shown. This may be cultural but could also be a protection from the sun.

Not everyone wears a tie. Safari suits are now worn only by drivers and the older people.

CHAPTER 8
Strategies for Business Success

Research the Market
Historically, the UAE market for consumer goods was divided into three segments. Marketers would target their products at UAE nationals; western expatriates from First World countries; and what were then called Third World nationals, expatriates from the subcontinent and other parts of Asia who had a lower socio-economic status. Today, the boundaries between these market segments have blurred. UAE nationals do not have quite the same disposable income they enjoyed in times gone by, western expatriates no longer occupy all the senior management positions, and subcontinent expatriates have moved into a number of senior management positions.

> **Don't Ignore the Bottom End of the Market**
> Visiting executives tend to conduct business in airconditioned offices and rely on resident executives to analyse the market rather than check out the market themselves.
>
> After launching a beverage product in the domestic market, a resident executive took the visiting executive to the better outlets. The field trip showed excellent distribution outlets for the product. However, market surveys revealed a low share of the market for the imported beverages. Only after patronising them, did the visiting executive learn that the dingy bars and one-star hotels was the market for his product. The reason for the low market share of the brand was lack of distribution effort. The resident executive and his sales team had not visited the low class outlets for fear of losing status!

Companies with healthy budgets can commission major international market research firms. A.C. Neilson has an office in Sharjah, and most major international accounting firms have research packages on specific markets through their offices in the UAE.

The UAE market for imported products may be too small for a full-scale market research. Low cost options for market research data include your country's chamber of commerce in the UAE or the commercial section of your country's diplomatic mission. These may be able to furnish you with basic data at a modest cost.

Befriending a UAE Camel to Make the Sale
An Australian exporter of stock feed visited the UAE with a view to supplying products to race camels owned by many UAE nationals. Most feed for race camels is imported from Saudi Arabia. Negotiations were moving slowly between the Australian feedstock supplier and the UAE government, the buyer. The Australian exporter decided to test his product directly with the race camels. He enlisted the help of his country's trade commission to make contact with the trainers of the race camels at their desert location. This initiative so impressed the UAE government that he was given two large orders, thereby costing the Saudis their exclusive supply.

The SME Strategy
The strategy for an Australian small to medium-sized business enterprise (SME) is to become part of an official Australian trade delegation. This facilitates networking opportunities, at a fairly high level, with businesses in the UAE and government. Alternatively, an Australian-based consultant who has worked in the UAE and is fluent in Gulf Arabic can be appointed to identify commercial organisations with the shortest distribution channels to reach the final consumer.

Although the number of western style retail stores is growing, traditional shops and markets known as souqs are still very much part of the retail scene. The most important souqs in Dubai include the gold souq, the textile souq, Al souq Al Kabeer (the big souq) and the spice souq. Supermarkets, department stores and regional shopping centres are displacing the traditional souq as markets for consumer goods. Regional shopping centres with their bargain prices and high quality merchandise even attract visiting tourists and Omanis, Qataris and Saudis who drive to Dubai to shop over the weekend. Buyers also come from as far afield as the CIS.

Embryonic supermarket chains include the British-based Spinneys, and the Indian-based Choitrams, Lifco and Lals. A French company is planning to open a hypermarket. New types of retail stores are opening. The Al Futtaim Trading Group, one of the largest corporations in the UAE, has launched *Plug Ins*, a chain of electronic super stores with outlets throughout the UAE.

A family shops for gold at the Sharjah Souk.

Gold is big consumer business. Two thirds of Dubai's citizens buy gold at least once a year. Half the gold purchased is given as a gift. Dubai has the densest concentration of gold shops—400 in all, 250 of which are located in the gold souq. In an area less than half a square kilometre, on any one day, 10 tonnes of gold are on display.

The Media

Radio
There are eight FM radio stations in the UAE, broadcasting in Arabic, English, Hindi and Urdu. Programmes broadcast in English follow the standard international format with a breakfast show, an afternoon show and the drive home show. Radio stations broadcasting in Arabic have a number of Muslim religious programmes, including an Islamic quiz and readings from the Koran. Most stations in all language groups are commercial stations supported by paid advertising.

Newspapers
There are nine daily newspapers: five are printed in Arabic and four in English. The two major English newspapers, the *Khaleej Times* and the *Gulf News*, have Arabic editions. Arabic language newspapers include *Al Bayan*, *Al Ittihad*, *Al Khaleej*, *Al Fajer* and *Al Wahda*.

Television
Abu Dhabi, Ajman, Dubai and Sharjah all have their own television channels telecasting in Arabic, English, Farsi and Urdu. In addition, one national broadcaster—*National Emirates TV*—broadcasts programmes of national interest in Arabic. Many TV viewers can also pick up programmes broadcast from Bahrain, Saudi Arabia and Qatar. Bahrain TV programmes are actually advertised in the local newspapers. Western expatriates have their favourite

programmes such as the *Bold and the Beautiful, Dr Quinn, Medicine Man* on the free to air television stations. Subcontinent expatriates also have the same opportunity as Indian films and serials are programmed. Telecasts in Arabic include films, news, cartoons and variety programmes. Muslim religious programmes, including readings from the Koran, and Islamic culture are a feature of Arabic telecasts. Complementing free to air television, is satellite pay TV.

English-speaking viewers have a wide selection of channels dedicated to movies, music, current affairs and sport. Subcontinent and Asian expatriates also have the opportunity to see a wide variety of programmes telecast in Urdu and other Asian languages. Nearly all residents have access to a TV set.

Outdoor Advertising

Outdoor advertising grew at 9% in 2001. High growth in road construction in Abu Dhabi, Sharjah and Dubai has resulted in new housing districts accompanied by a proliferation of signage. Billboard advertising is of a high professional standard.

McDonalds is everywhere, even in th UAE.

Trade Fairs and Exhibitions

The UAE is a major international and regional trade fair and exhibition centre, with well equipped facilities in each of the major cities. In the Emirate of Abu Dhabi, exhibitions are coordinated by the General Exhibition Corporation. In 2000, Abu Dhabi staged 14 significant exhibitions.

Dubai's World Trade Centre played a major role in organising more than 40 exhibitions in 2000. One of the major conferences in 2001 was the hosting of the Organisation of Economic Co-operation and Development's (OECD) Emerging Market Economy Forum. This was the first time the forum was held outside an OECD country.

Sharjah, not wanting to be left behind, commenced construction of a new expo centre in 2001. In line with its economic focus on the industrial sector, it is planning a number of commerce and industry shows. The Sharjah Chamber of Commerce will be responsible for Expo Centre Sharjah and the World Trade Centre project. There are also exhibition centres in Ras al Khaimah and Fujairah.

The UAE's Silicon Valley

In 2001, Dubai opened *Dubai Media City*, a precinct aimed at attracting investors and talent from the information technology industry. Dubai, like many places in the world, is trying to develop its Silicon Valley clone. The objective is to develop a computer software industry by developing the software writing skills of UAE and non UAE Arabs.

The first stage of Dubai Media City was completed in 2001, with 35 companies licensed to operate in the city. A number of pan Arab newspapers have offices in Dubai Media City for the distribution of their publications to the Gulf and the Middle East. A key player in the city is Emirates Media Corp, whose activities include print, broadcast and telecast. The city also has a Media Institute to train UAE nationals. Dubai Media City is also developing as a centre for the production of Indian music videos. The UAE Government censors output from Dubai Media City if material is for sale in the UAE. The monitoring authority is the Ministry for Information and Culture.

Dubai Media City has a strategic alliance with the Egyptian Media Production City based in Cairo. Incentives to locate in Dubai Media City include 100 % foreign ownership and 50-year corporate and personal income tax exemption.

Promotions and Marketing

By western standards, the UAE is a relatively unsophisticated market. Overseas suppliers of consumer goods usually provide their distributors with dealer material which includes show cards and brochures, and free stock for sampling. Retail marketing has all the hallmarks of those seen in the west. In the supermarket you will see in-pack and on-pack premiums and promotions; two for one consumer offers; bonus stock offers by distributors and wholesalers to retailers and supermarkets, in exchange for premium gondola display ends. The concept of brand loyalty and developing a brand franchise is evolving in the UAE. Most consumer products in the UAE require labelling in Arabic and English.

The Right Price

Business negotiations will most likely focus on price, margins and quality in that order. Whereas in the west there is more of a balance between quality and price (contracts not necessarily going to the lowest bidder), in the UAE price tends to be the key determinant. There are many instances where once a bidder has pre-qualified, the contract has been awarded to the lowest bidder.

A significant number of overseas suppliers have their products distributed by traders. Traders can usually make a quick sale for your product but they are not interested in developing your brand or a market for your product. The trader's main objective is to make a quick dirham through getting the lowest price out of you and selling to the highest bidder. Often the trader's profit margin is higher than yours despite the fact that it is you, the supplier, who have developed the product and taken most of the risk. The other major disadvantage of transacting with a trader is his lack of knowledge about the final consumer. You will have no market feedback to fine-tune your product.

The focus on price arises because, in the past, the country's main business activity was trading. Companies with western expatriates in senior management, may have a better understanding of building brands and developing a consumer franchise.

The Right Product

The UAE has historically looked to the UK, the US and Europe to source products and services. More recently, it is looking at other sources.

Quality Assurance

An Australian supplier of stock feed for camels was having a problem. Weevils infected the product when it arrived in the UAE. The weevil problem baffled the Australian supplier who reassured the UAE buyer that the product was free from weevils when it was shipped from Australia. Further investigations revealed that the weevils incubated while in transit. The supplier subsequently fixed the problem by sterilising the product before shipment but the UAE buyer insisted on a Quality Assurance Certification in accordance with international standards.

How an Australian Supplier of Trees, Plants and Shrubs was Able to Break into the US-dominated Market

An Australian supplier of trees, shrubs and plants was able to win a contract for some of the largest landscaping projects in the UAE. The Australian supplier sent his plants by air rather than by sea so that they arrived in a better condition than his competitors'.

> **Quality Assurance from the 4°C General Manager**
> The visiting general manager of a beverage company insisted on meeting bar staff dispensing his beverages to ensure that the delivery systems were hygienic and that the beverage was being dispensed at the correct temperature of 4° C. He achieved some notoriety by walking into bars, asking for the beverage, and then telling the barmen that the beverage was not cold enough. When the barmen protested, he whipped out a thermometer from his briefcase, stuck it into his glass and said, "See, not 4° C."
>
> **The International Beverage Manager's Six-month Trial**
> An international beverage company, which had been servicing the UAE and other Middle Eastern markets from Australia, decided to transfer its regional manager for the Middle East to the UAE for a six-month trial basis. The company calculated that the cost of relocating the manager and his family was about the same as the travel expenses they were paying, and the loss in travel days. The manager networked opportunities in the UAE that were not available in Australia, and was able to develop markets as far afield as Africa and Central Asia. The six-month trial was a success and his appointment was confirmed.

If your company wants to be a serious player in the UAE, you would need to open an office and have someone from your company, on the ground.

Commercial Laws of the UAE

The Commercial Agency Law

The Commercial Agency Law requires overseas companies to distribute their products through UAE nationals or enterprises and companies which are at least 51% owned by UAE nationals.

The Federal Companies Law

The Federal Companies Law applies to all commercial companies operating in the UAE, including branch offices of foreign companies. The law addresses requirements for establishing general partnerships, limited partnerships, share partnerships, joint venture companies, limited liability companies, publicly-held companies and private shareholding companies.

The Federal Industries Law

The Federal Industries Law requires that any industrial project must have 51% UAE ownership and UAE nationals must constitute the majority of the board. There are exemptions. Companies involved in small capital investment projects and those concerned with the oil and mineral industries are exempt.

Government Tender Law

Government projects are usually put out to tender. Under the Government Tender Law, there are often extensive regulations, particularly in Abu Dhabi, as to who can tender. The company awarded the tender will always be a company with at least 51% UAE ownership. This does not preclude an overseas company from entering into a joint venture with a UAE company.

Labour Laws

The UAE is a member of the International Labour Organisation (ILO) and is party to the convention protecting workers' rights. The laws specify employee entitlements in terms of annual leave, gratuities, medical benefits and provisions for repatriation.

Remuneration for working in the UAE usually includes a gratuity at the end of the contract. After one year of continuous service, the employee usually receives from the employer an additional 21 days' pay; after five years of continuous service, the employee normally receives an extra 30 days' pay each year.

Employment contracts must be registered. The Ministry of Labour and Social Affairs issues a standard labour contract for employees obtaining a work permit. Although all foreign employees have a standard labour contract, management staff usually have a much more comprehensive contract. The comprehensive contract will only stand up in law if it is consistent with UAE labour laws.

Market forces determine the remuneration of employees. There is no minimum wage but, in practice, the Ministry of Labour and Social Affairs will not approve a labour contract that is unfair or where the remuneration would not allow a minimum standard of living. Labour contracts must describe the cost of living allowances, transport arrangements, housing benefits and bonuses offered by employers to employees. Despite these provisions, there have been newspaper reports that free food has been supplied to some subcontinent expatriate workers in labour camps who find it difficult to make ends meet.

Trade unions are not permitted, and collective bargaining is prohibited. Strikes are unheard of and it is a criminal offence for civil servants to refuse to work.

Expatriates work in the UAE for economic reasons. Knowing that any sign of discontent with their employer can lead to termination and substantial loss of income, contributes to harmonious industrial relations in the UAE. Subcontinent expatriates in unskilled jobs can easily be replaced if they do not adhere to their employment contract terms. In the unlikely event of an employee being in dispute with his employer, there is a mechanism where the labour courts can appoint a conciliation committee.

The Ministry of Labour and Social Affairs is the agency that regulates labour laws. Other government agencies involved in the welfare of workers include the Ministry of Health (who sets health and safety standards), municipalities and civil defence units.

There is no child labour in the UAE. Employers cannot employ anybody under the age of fifteen, and special provisions apply to workers who are between the ages of fifteen and eighteen.

Although labour laws theoretically protect the employee, in practice, they are biased towards the employer. For example, a safety officer is required on a building site which employs more than 150 workers, but often the law is not enforced. When two laws relating to an employee are in conflict, labour laws will take precedence even if the other laws benefit the employee.

Intellectual Property Rights

The UAE has a good record for enforcing intellectual property laws. According to the Business Software Alliance (BSA), lost revenue through piracy in 1999 in the UAE was only 2% of the entire Middle East.

Case One

In July 1999, the Ministry of Information and Culture and the Dubai Police Economic Crime Section, on advice from the BSA, swooped down on video and CD shops in Dubai and the northern emirates. They confiscated and then destroyed thousands of pirated audio and video cassettes, compact discs and computer play-station tapes.

Case Two

As a result of an appeal by the Motion Picture Association of the Middle East, a trader who had been convicted of selling pirated video cassettes had his sentence increased from a fine of UAD 5,000 to a prison sentence of three months.

The UAE recognises the Paris Convention for the Protection of Industrial Property and the World Intellectual Property Organisation. It is a signatory to the World Trade Organisation's agreement on trade-related aspects of intellectual property. This protects copyrights, trademarks, patents, industrial designs and trade secrets. The UAE is also a party to the International Patent Co-operative Treaty of 1998 that protects inventions.

Within the UAE, intellectual property is protected by Federal Law number 40/92 and enforced by a number of UAE government agencies. The Ministry of Economy and Commerce enforces trademark registrations, the Ministry of Information and Culture enforces copyright law and the Ministry of Finance and Industry enforces patent and design law. Other government agencies assisting with intellectual property enforcement include the Ministry of Interior, Dubai's Department of Economic Development and Sharjah Municipality.

Business Licence

A business licence is required if you want to transact business in the UAE. If you appoint a commercial agent, a master distributor or a number of distributors, their business licence allows your product to be sold in the UAE. The chambers of commerce in each of the emirates usually issue business licences. There are a number of classes of business licences. They include trade licences, industrial licences, service licences, professional licences and construction licences. The issuing authority for the Emirate of Abu Dhabi is the Abu Dhabi Chamber of Commerce and Industry. They have been streamlining the way that business licences are issued. Where it once took up to four months for a licence to be issued, requests for trade or commercial licences can now be sent by e-mail and processed in one working day.

Company Registration

Having obtained a business licence, a company needs to be registered in the commercial register of, in the case of Dubai, the Ministry of Economy and Commerce. The information needed in the application form from the Ministry of Economy and Commerce of the Emirate of Dubai includes:

- Name of the company, its business activities and the countries where it trades. A company that trades with Israel is unlikely to get a licence.
- Description of business activities that the company will undertake in the UAE.
- Details of the service agent in the UAE, whether it is a UAE national or a UAE majority-owned company, and the service agent's address.

Documents to be submitted in support of the application include:
- An official certification from the authorities in the country where the foreign company is registered. This is to confirm that the company is operating in accordance with the law.
- A board minute indicating that the company has resolved to establish a business in the UAE and that the company representative in the UAE making the application has the power of attorney to act on behalf of the company. These letters need to be notarised by the government where the overseas company is located.
- The memorandum and articles of association of the company authenticated by the government of the country where the headquarters of the company is based, plus the last two audited balance sheets of the company.
- A copy of the legal agreement between the overseas company and the UAE service agent.
- The passport of the UAE service agent or, if it is a company, its emirate licensing details.

All documents submitted must be in Arabic. Translations must be certified.

In Dubai, the application form and supporting documentation will be referred to the committee of foreign companies at the Ministry of Economy and Commerce, which will approve the application and forward the application to the Minister of Economy and Commerce. If the Minister approves the application, the licence will be issued by the Department of Commercial Affairs within the Ministry.

The business licence is issued subject to the following conditions:
- An auditor be appointed if the company's name is on the chartered accountants register.
- Any changes in the company's business activity require changes to the business licence.
- The licence has to be renewed each year, one month before the expiry date.

Choosing a Business Site

Where you choose to locate in the UAE depends upon the nature of your business. If your business is associated with oil or oil-related products, then Abu Dhabi is the best location as it is home to the oil industry.

Abu Dhabi is dubbed the "Manhattan of the Middle East" because of its tall office buildings. It is the base for the banking, finance and telecommunications industries.

Dubai does not have the oil wealth of Abu Dhabi but it is very active in encouraging businesses to locate in the emirate. By far the most cosmopolitan centre in the UAE, Dubai has an international business outlook. If your business is in the service or trading sector, then Dubai, as the commercial capital of the UAE, is the best location. Prestigious business locations in Dubai include Shaikh Zayed Road where most of the banks are located.

In the UAE, offices and factories must be leased as only UAE nationals can own land. There are two components to leasing an office—the cost of actually leasing the office itself and the cost of leasing the adjacent areas and the service charges. The cost of leasing an office in Shaikh Zayed Road is UAD 55 per square foot

Dubai is a modern cosmopolitan city.

per year. There is a further charge of UAD 40 per square foot per year to cover the service charges associated with airconditioning, water, security and the public areas.

When setting up an office, it is important that the company projects a profitable image of its business. The principal of a major firm responsible for the interior design and décor of offices indicated that projecting a profitable image included having dark panelling and light coloured carpets for your office.

If you have regional management responsibilities beyond the UAE, Dubai is the best location as its airport is serviced by more international airlines than any other airport in the UAE.

The following table reflects precincts that the Dubai government has designated as Industrial Parks.

Industrial Parks—Dubai

Name	Hectares	Profiles
Al Khubaisi	102 hectars	Trading companies, warehousing, light industrial
Um Ramool	391 hectares	Warehousing and show rooms
Al Kuoz	1838 hectares	Warehousing and labour camps
Ras Al Khor	661 hectares	Small to medium-sized workshops and furniture factories
Al Safa	20 hectares	Factories producing food
Al Quasis	545 hectares	Construction and scrap metal industries, small to medium-sized industrial projects

Free Trade Zones and Technology Parks

Overview

Free trade zones generally offer their customers 100% foreign ownership, complete remittance of all profits, no corporate tax for fifteen years (renewable) and no income tax for employees. A not widely publicised disadvantage of locating in free trade zones is that, if you plan to export to other AGCC countries, you will not enjoy common market status (that is duty free) that applies to businesses actually operating in the UAE.

Dubai

The Jebel Ali Free Zone (JAFZ) This is by far the largest free trade zone. Located some 35 kilometres south west of Dubai, the

JAFZ houses one of the largest oilfield supply and distribution centres in the Middle East. Mina (meaning port) Jebel (meaning hill or mountain) Ali, with 67 berths, is the port for the JAFZ. It has also been given free trade zone status to facilitate the further development of re-exports from the Emirate of Dubai. Facilities at Mina Jebel Ali include modern container terminals and transit storage facilities that can be temperature-controlled.

JAFZ, established in 1985, was the first free trade zone in the Gulf. It allows foreign companies, complete ownership and duty free benefits. The JAFZ has the world's largest man-made harbour and is one of the world's largest industrial complexes. More than 1,600 companies from over 70 countries, and employing over 30,000 people, are based here. The free trade zone authority is the nominal employer of all labour. Many multinational companies use the JAFZ as their regional headquarters and distribution centre for the region. Manufacturing businesses in the zone tend to focus on textiles and final stage assembly of electronics.

The Dubai Department of Tourist and Commerce Marketing is responsible for promoting investments in the JAFZ.

Dubai Airport Free Zone Authority (DAFZA) DAFZA's objective is to attract international companies to make long term investments in projects that are not labour intensive but are environmentally friendly. In 1999, there were 50 companies operating in DAFZA, approximately half of which were from Europe and a third from the US. The types of businesses operating in the DAFZA include jewellery, crystal, diamonds, cosmetics and computer products.

Dubai Investment Park The planned Dubai Investment Park is a variation of the free trade zone concept. Companies locating in the park can have up to 75% foreign ownership instead of only 49% as required of businesses in Dubai. The benefit to investors is that, with 75% ownership, they have control of the company and the added benefit of being able to sell their products to AGCC countries, untaxed. The relaxation of foreign ownership rules is a result of the UAE needing to be competitive, with a Gulf trend to allow 75% foreign ownership.

Other Emirates

The Fujairah Free Trade Zone (FTZ) The FTZ has been growing at 20% per annum with 125 projects registered. The FTZ markets itself as offering business the locational advantage of an east coast port plus the opportunity to be in partnership with the Fujairah Government.

Hamriyyah Free Zone (HFZ) The HFZ located in Sharjah ncludes investments from other AGCC countries, as well as international companies. Approximately half the investment in the HFZ is from Sharjah-based enterprises.

Saadiyat Free Zone Authority (SFZA) In 1999, the SFZA gave Emirates Global Capital Corporation (EGCC) a fifty-year lease to develop Saadiyat Island, an island with nothing but sand and shrubs. This is the only free trade zone in Abu Dhabi, but it is still at concept stage, and not operational.

EGCC plans to develop a 50,000 sq m trading centre that will include a stock exchange, a commodities exchange and an offshore banking centre. Plans are also afoot to build a port and a freight airport. Included in the zone will be residential properties, a marina, an exhibition centre plus a luxury hotel with a golf course. The zone is planned to be linked to Abu Dhabi city via a six-lane bridge. Complementing the commodities exchange is a plan to provide a physical storage centre for commodities shipped between Asia and Europe.

This development is to lessen Abu Dhabi's dependence on oil, and to enhance private investment in the emirate. Companies operating in the zone are offered repatriation of all their profits and capital as an incentive. In fact, the government has even announced that companies with offices on Saadiyat Island need never pay tax. Further incentives include allowing foreign participants 100% ownership. The Abu Dhabi Government hopes that the foreign private sector will invest in the project. Despite elaborate plans, as at 2001, the project was only at concept stage.

Ras al Khaimah Free Zone　Like the other emirates, Ras al Khaimah is developing its free trade zone to attract more businesses to diversify its economy.

Ajman Information Technology Park (AITP)　The Ajman Free Zone whose business included textiles, medical equipment, furniture, food, tobacco derivatives, watches, electrical appliances and metal products, developed into the AITP. The strategy of the AITP is to offer a *move in and plug in* service to IT developers and companies involved in e-commerce and internet wholesaling and retailing.

Sharjah is the base for the manufacturing industry. Office space and housing rentals are lower than in Abu Dhabi and Dubai, and because of the added benefit of easy commuting from Sharjah to Dubai, one can live in Sharjah and work in Dubai.

One of the most frustrating aspects of setting up a business in the UAE is the amount of documentation needed for even the most simple business requirement. For example, if you want to have your telephone connected, you have to show the telephone company a "no objection' letter from your landlord plus the tenancy agreement.

> **The Documents Pack**
> One of the problems of obtaining business services is that you are never sure what documents will be required. One expatriate general manager created a documents pack that he took with him whenever he required a business service. Among the items included in the pack were many passport-sized photographs of himself, his wife and children (you need a photo for almost anything), all the "no objection" letters, his birth certificate, marriage certificate, resident certificate, work permit, employment contract, health card and certificates of his academic qualifications. All these documents were attested by his country's embassy in the UAE.

The government will bend over backwards to assist you in recruiting a UAE national and has programmes such as the Public Authority for National Development and Employment, established in 1999, that matches employers' needs to UAE nationals' capabilities. Employers can also list job vacancies on the Ministry of Labour and Social Affairs job website.

> **January 2001**
> **Indicative Average Monthly Salaries UAD**
>
> | | |
> |---|---:|
> | Junior nurse | 3,000 |
> | Subcontinent or Asian expatriate secretaries/ PA | 3,500 |
> | Sheet and metal fabricator | 950 |
> | Arab sales manager | 20,000 |
> | Business development manager | 20,000 |
> | Secretary (UK/US) | 6,000 |
> | IT supervisor (Filipino/Chinese) | 8,000 |
> | Storekeeper | 3,000 |
> | Software development engineer | 12,000 |

If you recruit a UAE national, you will have to offer the same generous social security and pension benefits that the government offers.

Contacts and Networking

Business executives should network with the three different groups in the UAE. If you are a western expatriate dealing with companies managed by western expatriates, your sports and social activities will provide you with a number of opportunities. Formal functions such as lunches or dinners are hosted by foreign chambers of commerce which include the ABIG (Australian Business In the Gulf) and BIG (British Business in the Gulf).

Functions arranged by the individual emirate chambers of commerce will also provide you with opportunities to meet the other two levels of networking—UAE nationals and subcontinent and Asian expatriates.

Corporate Culture

The chairmen of major UAE companies are often members of the royal family. They are customarily shown more deference and subservience by employees than the chairman of a western company. For example in western culture, the chairman is often addressed by his or her first name whereas in the UAE, the relationship is more formal. Job titles in major UAE companies tend to follow the UK model where executives are designated as general manager or managing director, rather than the US system of president and vice president.

A feature in all businesses and government offices is a framed photograph of the president of the UAE and a framed photograph of the ruler of the emirate where the business is located. The two photographs will be located in a prominent place such as the foyer or in the board room. Often, if the company is a foreign joint venture, there will be a framed photograph of the head of state of the foreign company. So, a British joint venture company with an office in Dubai, would probably have a framed photograph of the queen, the president of the UAE and the ruler of Dubai.

A few major companies, like the Emirates Group, provide incentives to employees through a profit sharing programme.

Like the Japanese, UAE nationals tend to stay with the one organisation—usually the government—throughout their corporate life. Smaller UAE companies practise nepotism because UAE executives believe that they must look after their extended family. They also believe that relatives in senior management positions will not steal from the company because that would mean stealing from the family and themselves.

Whereas executives in western-style corporations separate business friendships from social friendships, executives who are UAE nationals tend to blend the two. This is most pronounced in smaller UAE companies.

Like western corporations, larger UAE companies have a management level with different functions from the board of directors. They are empowered with specific functions such as financial matters. Senior managers in larger UAE companies are accustomed to debating issues with their bosses. Junior managers and supervisory staff, often expatriates from the subcontinent, do not join in these debates because they feel questioning their superior's decisions may lead to dismissal. For the same reason, supervisors do not like to convey bad news to their superiors.

UAE small business offices are not renovated in the same style as large corporations. They are less ready to spend money on office renovations as they feel that office image is less important. A feature of the *outer* office in a UAE owned and managed, small to medium-sized business, is the way that the non managerial staff desks are arranged together to save space and cost.

In your business negotiations, remember that your staff are likely to be subcontinent expatriates who usually thrive on gossip. The employment of secretaries or personal assistants in the UAE is price-driven but if you employ someone from Europe, South

Africa, Australia or the US, you may pay more but your business remains private.

Personnel practices of UAE-owned and managed corporations differ from those of western companies where the job is defined and the right person is found to fill it. In the UAE, companies create jobs for their friends and family members. Also, executives who are UAE nationals enjoy greater job security than expatriate managers.

> **Tell Your Employees That You Want to Know Both the Good News and the Bad**
> There is a tendency for subcontinent expatriate employees to tell only the good news to their bosses. They believe that telling bad news could lead to the loss of their jobs.

Conclusion

The UAE is the fastest developing economy of all the AGCC countries. Although oil and gas remain the principal source of income, the government has been pro-active in diversifying the economy through making its non oil sectors attractive to investors.

It is becoming more of a market economy as evidenced by the fairly recent establishment of a stock exchange, the reduction of red tape and the updating of its commercial laws and regulations.

With an excellent infrastructure for business, and good transport and communications network, the UAE is the gateway to the Gulf for distribution and re-export of goods into the region. Other business incentives include no revenue and exchange controls, the absence of taxes, and a large multinational expatriate work force.

APPENDIX A

Basic Facts and Travel Tips

Location
The United Arab Emirates is located along the eastern coast of the Arabian Peninsula. It has 1,000 kilometres (620 miles) of coastline on the Arabian Gulf and 130 kilometres (80 miles) of coastline on the Gulf of Oman. The seven emirates that make up the union are bordered by Qatar on the west, Oman on the south and northeast, and Saudi Arabia on the south and west. The area of the UAE is 83,600 square kilometres (33,400 square miles). The capital is Abu Dhabi city.

Climate
The UAE is known for its blue skies and year-round sunshine. The best time to visit the country is between November and March when the UAE experiences warm sunny days and cool nights, with an average temperature of 18° C (65° F). High temperatures of up to 50° C (122° F) and high humidity are experienced in summer, between April and September, with sand storms from the southerly and northerly winds. Climatic conditions vary between the coastal regions, the deserts and the mountain regions. Rainfall averages 75 mm to 100mm (3 to 4 inches) annually.

Topography
Most of the UAE is sandy desert with extensive salt flats less than 150 metres (500 feet) above sea level. The Al Hajar Mountains in eastern UAE rise to 3,050 metres (10,000 feet) above sea level.

The UAE has a number off shore islands and coral reefs.

Passports
Visitors to the UAE require a valid passport and a visa. Citizens

and expatriate residents of AGCC are exempt from visa requirements, as are British citizens with right of abode in the UK. Visas must be applied for before entering the UAE.

There are two types of tourist visas—visit visas and transit visas. A visit visa must be sponsored by a company operating in the UAE. It is valid for two months from the date of arrival, and renewable for another month. A transit visa is valid for 14 days and cannot be renewed. If you overstay your visit visa, a ten-day grace period is allowed for you to leave the country, after which a fine is imposed for every day you overstay.

Security

Media stories from the Middle East conjure up images of violence from Lebanon, the Palestinian problem and the difficult living conditions in Saudi Arabia where western women have to abide by a strict dress standard and cannot drive cars. Exercise common sense, and you will find the UAE a safe place to live in.

Modern Health and Welfare System

UAE nationals enjoy an excellent free health and welfare system, but this benefit is not available to foreigners who will be charged for health care. A weakness in the health system is that when doctors prescribe tests, the laboratories sometimes take longer than in the west to analyse the results, delaying further treatment

Western and other expatriates who can afford to wait have a choice of 14 private hospitals that include the American hospital or the Indian based Lal Khaleej Medical Centre, both based in Dubai.

Most doctors and nurses are expatriates from the subcontinent and Asia. The UAE Ministry of Health regularly invites foreign medical specialists to visit the 35 public hospitals and 128 outpatient clinics in the UAE. The 2001 programme invited specialist doctors from Europe, the US and Egypt to visit the Al Jazira, Al Mafraq and Al Qassimi hospitals to consult in areas that included paediatrics, vascular medicine, sports medicine and neurosurgery.

Recent statistics indicate that there is one medical practitioner for every 697 persons. Mortality rates are 20 deaths per 1,000 live births. Approximately 2% to 3% of GDP is spent on health care.

Currently, the UAE government subsidises the cost of health care for UAE nationals. As with electricity, the government wants to reduce its exposure to subsidies. The federal government and the government of the Emirate of Abu Dhabi have taken the first steps to privatise health care. Their strategy is to work with the UAE Offset Group (UOG) to launch the Emirate Health Care Company.

Shopping

The UAE and, in particular, Dubai is often said to be a shoppers' paradise where there is the option of visiting the traditional markets known as souqs or the modern shopping malls. The best time to visit Dubai for bargains is in March where there is the month-long Dubai shopping festival and in June, July and August when there are Dubai summer surprises.

The Gold Souq

Dubai is known as the city of gold and is famous for its many shops selling gold. Unlike in the west where pieces of jewellery are sold at retail for a set price, gold is sold by weight. So when you buy a gold chain, the merchant first puts the piece on the scales and then tells you the price.

The Sharjah Souqs

Sharjah has two major souqs (regional shopping centres) that are distinctive landmarks.

Gourmet Food Stores
There are many stores in Dubai selling saffron and reasonably priced caviar from Iran.

Religion
The official religion is Islam as nearly all UAE nationals are Muslims mainly of the Sunni sect. The Government permits the worshipping of other religions and there are Christian churches in Abu Dhabi, Dubai and Sharjah.

Language
The official language is Arabic and UAE nationals speak a Gulf dialect. English is widely spoken and business visitors may attend numerous meetings without hearing Arabic. Other languages frequently spoken include Hindi, Farsi and Urdu.

APPENDIX B

Directory of Important Contacts

Abu Dhabi Chamber of Commerce and Industry
P.O. Box 662, Abu Dhabi, UAE.
Tel: 971 221 4000
Fax: 971 2 786 766

Abu Dhabi Municipality
P.O. Box 263, Abu Dhabi, UAE.
Tel: 971 278 888
Fax: 971 2 786 766

Ajman Chamber of Commerce and Industry
P.O. Box 662, Ajman, UAE.
Tel: 971 6 422 177

Australian Business in the Gulf (ABIG)
P.O. Box 20183, Dubai, UAE.
Tel: 971 4 265 2781
Fax: 971 4 265 2761
Email: abigdxb@emirates.net.ae

Austrade, The Australian Consulate General
P.O. Box 9303, UAE.
Tel: 971 4 331 3444
Fax: 971 4 331 4812
www.austrade.gov.au

Dubai Chamber of Commerce and Industry
P.O. Box 1457, Dubai, UAE.
Tel: 971 4 280 000
Fax: 971 4 211 646

Dubai Municipality
P.O. Box 67, Dubai, UAE.
Tel: 971 4 221 141
Fax: 971 4 231 795

Department of Economic Development
P.O. Box 13223, Dubai, UAE.
Tel: 971 4 229 922
Fax: 971 4 2254 577

The Economic Department
P.O. Box 853, Abu Dhabi, UAE.
Tel: 971 2 318 800
Fax: 971 2318 970

Federal Ministry of Economy and Commerce
P.O. Box 3625, Dubai, UAE.
Tel: 971 4 284 151
Fax: 971 4 225 685

Federal Ministry of Finance and Industry
P.O. Box 1565, Dubai, UAE.
Tel: 971 4 532 323
Fax: 971 4 530 571

Federation of UAE Chambers of Commerce and Industry
P.O. Box 8886, Dubai, UAE.
Tel: 971 4 212 977
Fax: 971 4 235 498

Fujairah Chamber of Commerce and Industry
P.O. Box 738, Fujairah, UAE.
Tel: 971 9 222 400

Government of Dubai
Department of Tourism and Commerce Marketing
P.O. Box 594, Dubai, UAE.
Tel: 971 4 511 600
Fax: 971 4 511 711
Internet: http://www.dctpb.gov.ae/
Email: info@dubaitourism.co.ae

Jebel Ali Free Zone Authority
P.O. Box 17000, Dubai, UAE.
Tel: 971 4 815 000
Fax: 971 4 816 093

Ras al Khaimah Chamber of Commerce and Industry
P.O. Box 87, Ras al Khaimah, UAE.
Tel: 971 7 333 511

Sharjah Chamber of Commerce and Industry
P.O. Box 580, Sharjah, UAE.
Tel: 971 6 541 444

Umm al Qaiwain Chamber of Commerce and Industry
P.O. Box 436, Umm al Qaiwain, UAE.
Tel: 971 6 656 915

APPENDIX C

Recommended Reading

Codrai, Ronald. *Abu Dhabi—An Arabian Album 1997* (Motivate Publishing, Dubai).

Fairservice, Ian. *Dubai, Gateway to the Gulf* (Motivate Publishing, Dubai, 1999).

Fairservice, Ian and Demangeot, Catherine. *Dubai, a Pictorial Tour 1999* (Motivate Publishing, Dubai).

Fairservice, Ian; Demangeot, Catherine & John, Kate. *Abu Dhabi, Life and Times* (Motivate Publishing, Dubai).

Hellyer, Peter and Fairservice, Ian. *Abu Dhabi, Garden City of the Gulf* (Motivate Publishing, Dubai).

Hellyer, Peter and Buckton, Rosalind. *Al Ain, Oasis City* (Motivate Publishing, 1998).

Kay, Shirley. *Land of the Emirates* (Motivate Publishing, Dubai, 19990.

Kay Shirley. *Portrait of Ras al Khaimah* (Motivate Publishing, Dubai, 1994).

Novell, John. *A Day Above the Emirates* (Motivate Publishing, Dubai, 1997).

National Corporation for Tourism and Hotels. Abu Dhabi, a Pictorial Tour (Motivate Publishing, Dubai, 1998).

Noor Ali Rashid. *The UAE Vision of Change* (Motivate Publishing, Dubai, 1999).

Noor Ali Rashid. *Dubai, Life and Times* (Motivate Publishing, Dubai, 1997).

Williams, Jeremy. *Cross-cultural Considerations for Business and Life in the Gulf* (Business Books, an imprint of Motivate Publishing, Dubai, 1998).

About the Authors

HARVEY TRIPP, a graduate of the University of Melbourne, spent most of his corporate life in international business. He has held senior management positions in major international consumer goods companies including the management of their operations in the United Arab Emirates(UAE). Harvey has lectured on international business, including how to do business in the UAE, at a number of universities in Australia and has been on university and other tertiary institutions' advisory boards to help develop their international business programmes.

Harvey has been a consultant to small and medium-sized businesses and has had interim executive assignments with corporations whose primary focus is on international business. He has also been a director of small to medium-sized Australian companies.

He is the co-author of *Culture Shock—Success Secrets to Maximize Business in Hong Kong*.

MARGARET TRIPP, a graduate of Deakin University, is a member of the senior management team at a leading high school in Australia that focuses on attracting overseas students.

Margaret has travelled extensively throughout the Middle East, including the United Arab Emirates, and has met with senior members of the business community. She has a sound understanding of how business is conducted and the cultural aspects of life in the UAE.

Margaret has been a board member of a small to medium-sized Australian company. She co-authored *Culture Shock—Success Secrets to Maximize Business in Hong Kong*, and currently writes articles for a quarterly magazine.

Index

abras 72
Abu Dhabi 11-19, 21, 22, 25, 32-34, 37, 38, 43-47, 52, 53, 55, 61, 63, 65, 66, 70, 71, 73, 87, 97, 98, 100, 101, 103, 104, 106-108, 110, 112, 116, 117, 122, 159, 160, 168, 170, 174, 175, 182, 183
Abu Dhabi Chamber of Commerce and Industry 58, 59
Abu Dhabi Fund for Development 31
Abu Dhabi Investment Authority 31, 34
Abu Dhabi Islamic Bank 131
Abu Dhabi National Hotels Corporation (ADNHC) 142
Abu Dhabi National Oil Company (ADNOC) 17, 18, 21, 22, 23, 61
accommodation 82, 85
agriculture 96-98
airlines 68
airports 65,
Ajman 12, 16, 25, 34, 54, 70, 98, 105, 110, 159, 175
Al Ain 11, 53, 58, 65, 80, 95, 97, 103, 108

alcohol 122, 133, 143, 145, 150, 151
Amex 78
Arab Bank for Investment & Foreign Trade 30
Arab Gulf Co-operation Council (AGCC) 23, 24, 26, 30, 32, 35, 42, 50, 58, 62, 70, 76, 85, 91, 102, 107, 108, 113, 116, 123, 128, 172, 174, 179
Arab League 50
Arab Monetary Fund 30
Asia 26, 101
Australia 62, 79, 82, 94, 106, 117, 128, 140, 157, 163, 164, 179

Bahrain 13, 16, 23, 26, 30, 42, 43, 45, 69, 159
Bangladesh 35
banks 30, 31, 170
branch office 121-24
bribery 143, 144
British Protectorate 12
Burj al Arab 28, 111, 147
buses 70
business
   agent/distributor 116, 118, 119, 128, 168
   appointments 139
   cards 149

culture 130, 131, 138, 139, 140, 143, 148, 149-50, 171, 177
dress 154, 155
entertainment 150, 151
exclusivity 119
hours 153, 154
licence 168
meetings 56, 138, 150, 151
partner 115, 116, 120
registration 168-70
site 170, 171
sponsors 119, 121, 122

cars 72
chamber of commerce 58, 59, 60, 122
China 35
civil service 55-57, 136
commercial agency law 128, 129
commercial transaction law 128, 129
Commonwealth of Independent States (CIS) 26, 37, 67
courier service 78
currency 29, 30

defence 112-14
dhows 11, 28, 62, 105
dirham 29, 30
DNATA 68, 80, 81, 92, 103
driving 85-87
Dubai 12, 16, 19, 21, 22, 25-29, 32-34, 37, 38, 43, 45, 47, 53-55, 61-66, 70-73, 83, 84, 86, 87, 92, 95, 100-02, 105-08, 110, 111, 116, 122, 124, 132, 136, 147, 158-60, 167, 168, 170-75, 178, 182, 183
Dubai Aluminium Company (Dubal) 74, 89, 107
Dubai Chamber of Commerce and Industry 59
Dubai Media City 161
Dubai Petroleum Company 19
Dubai World Cup 89
duty free 101, 103, 147, 172

economy 11, 25
education 78, 79, 80, 81, 82, 135
electricity 73, 74
Emirates Airlines 41, 68, 81, 92, 103, 118, 154
Emirates Group 41, 102, 103, 161, 178
Emirates National Oil Company (ENOC) 19
Emirates Telecommunications Corporation (Etisalat) 42, 76, 77
emirs 55
employment contract 36, 127, 166, 167, 177
Europe 19, 163, 179
exhibitions 59, 112, 161
exports 26-29

Federal National Council 48
federation 14
fishing 12, 99, 100
France 19, 102
free trade zone 120, 123, 172-75
Fujairah 16, 17, 22, 25, 54, 63,

    65, 68, 74, 94, 98, 100, 102, 103, 174

gas 21-22
gold 26, 146, 158, 159
government
  emirate 44, 45, 47, 48, 52-55
  federal 32, 44, 45, 47, 55
Gulf Air 68, 69, 70, 128
Gulf Aircraft Maintenance Company (GAMCO) 70
Gulf War 16

Hatta 101, 103
health 181, 182
Hong Kong 26, 28, 65, 67, 69, 102

immigration 92, 93
imports 26-29
India 26, 35
industries 94-114
  construction 111
  consumer goods 109
  film 105, 106
  food 95-100
  manufacturing 106
  quarrying 94
  shipbuilding and repairing 104
  travel and tourism 101
International Labour Organisation (ILO) 165
International Petroleum Investment Company 19
Iran 43, 50, 69, 107
Iraq 50

Israel 30, 51, 92, 93, 114, 169

Japan 19, 21, 102, 107, 178
Jebel Ali Free Zone 19, 72, 95, 106, 110, 173
joint ventures 122, 123, 124
judiciary 48-50

KFOR 113
Korea 35
Kuwait 20, 23, 26, 45, 50, 62, 102, 113

language 56, 65, 129, 139, 159, 160, 162, 169, 183
legal system 48-50, 120, 121, 124, 125, 164-67
limousines 70

Majlis 51
media 159-62

NATO 113

OAPEC 20
OECD 161
oil 13, 17-20, 170
Oman 23, 62
OPEC 20

Pakistan 19, 26, 35
Pakistan International Airlines 65
partnerships 125
pearling 12
Philippines 35
pirate coast 11, 12, 29

ports 29, 61
postal service 77, 78

Qatar 23, 62, 159

Ramadan 44, 154-55
Ras al Khaimah 11, 12, 16, 17, 20, 22, 25, 37, 54, 63, 65, 68, 94, 96, 99, 102, 103, 107, 108, 110, 174, 175
re-exports 26, 179
religion 130, 131, 133, 154, 155, 159, 160, 183
representative office 123
roads 63, 64

safety 90
Saudi Arabia 20, 23, 26, 62, 85, 102, 113, 159
Shaikh Maktoum 47, 53
Shaikh Mohammed 52, 53
Shaikh Zayed 46, 52
Sharjah 16, 20, 22, 33, 47, 54, 55, 63, 65, 67, 68, 70, 73, 82, 84, 95, 100-02, 104, 106, 110, 116, 117, 122, 157, 159, 160, 168, 174, 175, 183
shopping 18, 182-83
Singapore 26, 28, 29, 35, 66, 69, 105
souq 31, 102, 141, 158, 182, 183
sponsorship 33, 35, 57, 91, 115, 121-23, 125-28
sports 89, 90
Sri Lanka 35
stock exchange 32

subsidies 73, 75
Supreme Petroleum Council 18

tariffs 32, 33
Taweelah power plant 73
taxes 32, 33, 79
taxis 70
technology parks 41, 120, 172-75
telecommunications 76, 77, 170
tourism 136
trade fairs 161
Trucial States 12-14, 63

UAE Offset Group 21, 22, 104, 108, 113, 114, 182
Umm al Qaiwain 16, 25, 54, 55, 63, 96, 100
UK 11, 12, 14, 19, 58, 85, 91, 94, 102, 116, 117, 163, 177
US 19, 26, 49, 50, 58, 79, 81, 102, 104, 107, 108, 111, 114, 117, 130, 163, 177, 179

visas 36, 78, 91, 120, 123, 125, 126, 127, 180, 181

walis 55
water 74
women 37, 80, 82, 86, 134-37, 149, 155, 181
work force 34-42
World Trade Organisation (WTO) 57, 167
World War I 12